Testing in the Schools

Walter E. Hathaway, *Editor*

NEW DIRECTIONS FOR TESTING AND MEASUREMENT
MICHAEL KEAN, *Editor-in-Chief*

Number 19, September 1983

Paperback sourcebooks in
The Jossey-Bass Social and Behavioral Sciences Series

Jossey-Bass Inc., Publishers
San Francisco • Washington • London

Walter E. Hathaway (Ed.).
Testing in the Schools.
New Directions for Testing and Measurement, no. 19.
San Francisco: Jossey-Bass, 1983.

New Directions for Testing and Measurement Series
Michael Kean, *Editor-in-Chief*

New Directions for Testing and Measurement is published
quarterly by Jossey-Bass Inc., Publishers. Subscriptions, single-issue
orders, change of address notices, undelivered copies, and other
correspondence should be sent to *New Directions* Subscriptions,
Jossey-Bass Inc., Publishers, 433 California Street, San Francisco,
California 94104.

Editorial correspondence should be sent to the Editor-in-Chief,
Michael Kean, ETS, Evanston, Illinois 60201.

Library of Congress Catalogue Card Number LC 82-84214
International Standard Serial Number ISSN 0271-0609
International Standard Book Number ISBN 87589-975-7

Cover art by Willi Baum
Manufactured in the United States of America

Ordering Information

The paperback sourcebooks listed below are published quarterly and can be ordered either by subscription or single-copy.

Subscriptions cost $35.00 per year for institutions, agencies, and libraries. Individuals can subscribe at the special rate of $21.00 per year *if payment is by personal check.* (Note that the full rate of $35.00 applies if payment is by institutional check, even if the subscription is designated for an individual.) Standing orders are accepted. Subscriptions normally begin with the first of the four sourcebooks in the current publication year of the series. When ordering, please indicate if you prefer your subscription to begin with the first issue of the *coming* year.

Single copies are available at $7.95 when payment accompanies order, and *all single-copy orders under $25.00 must include payment.* (California, New Jersey, New York, and Washington, D.C., residents please include appropriate sales tax.) For billed orders, cost per copy is $7.95 plus postage and handling. (Prices subject to change without notice.)

Bulk orders (ten or more copies) of any individual sourcebook are available at the following discounted prices: 10–49 copies, $7.15 each; 50–100 copies, $6.35 each; over 100 copies, *inquire.* Sales tax and postage and handling charges apply as for single copy orders.

To ensure correct and prompt delivery, all orders must give either the *name of an individual* or an *official purchase order number.* Please submit your order as follows:

Subscriptions: specify series and year subscription is to begin.
Single Copies: specify sourcebook code (such as, TM8) and first two words of title.

Mail orders for United States and Possessions, Latin America, Canada, Japan, Australia, and New Zealand to:
Jossey-Bass Inc., Publishers
433 California Street
San Francisco, California 94104

Mail orders for all other parts of the world to:
Jossey-Bass Limited
28 Banner Street
London EC1Y 8QE

New Directions for Testing and Measurement Series
Michael Kean, *Editor-in-Chief*

TM1 *Measurement and Educational Policy,* William B. Schrader
TM2 *Insights from Large-Scale Surveys,* John E. Milholland
TM3 *Impactive Changes on Measurement,* Roger T. Lennon
TM4 *Methodological Developments,* Ross E. Traub
TM5 *Measuring Achievement: Progress over a Decade,* William B. Schrader

TM6 *Interpreting Test Performance,* Samuel T. Mayo
TM7 *Recent Developments in Affective Measurement,* David A. Payne
TM8 *Measurement Aspects of Title I Evaluations,* Gary Echternacht
TM9 *Admissions Testing and the Public Interest,* William B. Schrader
TM10 *Testing in the States: Beyond Accountability,* Dale Carlson
TM11 *Issues in Testing: Coaching, Disclosure, and Ethnic Bias,* Bert F. Green
TM12 *Measuring Human Abilities,* Philip Merrifield
TM13 *Measurement, Guidance, and Program Improvement,* William Schrader
TM14 *Impact of Desegregation,* Daniel J. Monti
TM15 *Productivity Assessment in Education,* Anita A. Summers
TM16 *Academic Testing and the Consumer,* Scarvia B. Anderson, Louisa V. Coburn
TM17 *Measurement, Technology, and Individuality in Education,* Ruth B. Ekstrom
TM18 *Generalizability Theory: Inferences and Practical Applications,* Leslie J. Fyans, Jr.

Contents

Editor's Notes   1
Walter E. Hathaway

Foreword   5
Matthew Prophet

Chapter 1. Uses of Testing in the Schools: A National Profile   7
Joan L. Herman, Donald W. Dorr-Bremme
This chapter provides information on the wide variety of tests used in the schools. It describes the purposes for which principals and teachers employ test results and their feelings about how successful test data are in helping them to meet their goals.

Chapter 2. Preparing Students for Standardized Testing   19
Glynn D. Ligon
Testing professionals need to work with teaching staff and parents to help students prepare for standardized testing. One prescription for dealing with this key concern of students, teachers, and parents is offered here.

Chapter 3. Teacher-Made Tests: Windows on the Classroom   29
Margaret Fleming, Barbara Chambers
Teacher-made tests are a major but little researched part of the drama of testing in schools and classrooms. This chapter gives a view into the inner workings of this aspect of testing, which occupies more teacher and student time and effort than any other.

Chapter 4. Testing and the Minority Child   39
Leonard C. Beckum
Much of the debate on testing over the last two decades has centered on issues of equity. In this review of testing and the minority child, the ways in which we can test and use test results to help all children learn are explained.

Chapter 5. Introduction to Latent Trait Analysis and   49
Item Response Theory
Joseph P. Ryan
One of the major theoretical and practical developments in testing is latent trait analysis and item response theory. This chapter provides a guide for practitioners in understanding, evaluating, and using these developments to meet their testing needs.

Chapter 6. Applications of Microcomputers to Classroom Testing   65
Ronald K. Hambleton, G. Ernest Anderson, Linda N. Murray
Microcomputer technology is perhaps the most exciting topic for school people today. This review of applications of such new technology provides a helpful road map to the present and future possibilities that the small computer is opening up for testing in the schools.

Chapter 7. A Case Study: Testing in the Albuquerque Public Schools   79
Carol Robinson
This case study highlights improvement of test results dissemination and use through cooperative planning, integrated data base development, and a partnership with public media.

Chapter 8. A Case Study: Testing in the   85
Los Angeles Public Schools
Floraline Stevens, Marilyn Burns
This case study illustrates ways to successfully meet the challenge of the complexity of test programs and testing scheduling in a large and diverse school system.

Chapter 9. A Case Study: Testing in the Dallas   91
Independent School District
Cordelia R. Alexander
This case study illuminates ways in which the testing program can support a district-wide instructional improvement process and formation of a network of building test coordinators.

Chapter 10. A Case Study: Testing in the Austin   97
Independent School District
Glynn D. Ligon, M. Kevin Matter
This case study describes how the philosophy and staffing of a testing program can work together to produce effective results with highly efficient use of student time and minimal clerical burden on teaching staff.

Chapter 11. A Case Study: Testing in the State of Mississippi   103
Thomas H. Saterfiel
This case study shows how testing can be used as an effective part of a statewide accountability and instructional improvement program.

Index   111

Editor's Notes

Today testing is taken more seriously by American schools and school systems than it ever was before. There was a hiatus in the steady growth of testing during the late 1960s and early to mid 1970s, when many became discouraged by the apparent inequities and limitations of tests and by confusion over the nature and value of the standards on which tests reported. But, in the last decade, an irresistible set of forces has converged to press testing onward once again. The back-to-basics movement; the quest to improve standards and accountability in the face of dwindling resources and support; the research on effective schools and classrooms, with its emphasis on clear, high academic expectations and prompt, accurate knowledge of results; and many other factors have all combined to make testing once again one of the highest priorities for school people and their clients. This *New Directions in Testing and Measurement* sourcebook on testing in the schools examines the ways in which the education and measurement communities are rising to the challenge posed by rediscovery of the potential value and importance of tests, including criterion- and curriculum-referenced measures, item banking, computer-based testing and reporting, the new emphasis on teacher measurement and test use skills, latent trait methodology, competence measures, and new approaches to ensuring equity.

One major aspect of the renewed commitment to testing is recognition of the primacy of the classroom as the focus for testing and test use. Teachers need to know what parts of the planned curriculum their students understand and can master and what parts they cannot. Hence, we see a strong, new emphasis on helping teachers to develop and extend their classroom observation and testing skills. Moreover, teachers are willing, even eager to collaborate in efforts to gather valid and reliable test data, because such data can help them to identify and meet their students' needs. This new emphasis places the previously dominant needs of administrators and policy makers in a dependent and subordinate position, and it is a source of great grassroots strength for the current renewal in testing.

Many new developments in testing, such as the curriculum, criterion, and competence measurement agendas have their greatest impetus at the state and local school system level. But, there is renewed vigor and diversity in the testing industry as well, which builds on the solid base of the past in such new developments as testing tailored to system, school, teacher, and student needs and support by item banking, latent trait linking, and computer technology.

All these issues and developments and many more are addressed in this volume by people who are responsible for testing in school systems and by

1

those to whom they turn for help. In discussing their individual topics, many authors have given voice to the most important link in the testing–learning chain that stretches between test and student, namely the classroom teacher, but the other key voices — measurement theorists and researchers, test developers, school administrators, parents, and many others — are heard and woven into the chorus calling for more and better testing and pointing to ways forward while raising cautions along the way.

In Chapter One, Joan Herman and Donald Dorr-Bremme make an in-depth report on how the results of the wide variety of tests in use today actually affect schools. The three-year study just completed by the Center for the Study of Evaluation provides information on the purposes for which principals and teachers employ test results and on their feelings about how successful test data are in helping them to meet their goals.

In Chapter Two, Glynn Ligon describes how she and her colleagues in Austin, Texas, work with staff and parents to help students prepare for standardized testing. She offers an insightful prescription for dealing with this key concern of students, teachers, and parents as tests grow in importance.

Next, we turn to the Cleveland city schools for a discussion by Margaret Fleming and Barbara Chambers of the strengths and limitations of a major but little-researched part of the drama of testing in schools and classrooms: teacher-made tests. Their report gives a powerful and much-needed view into the inner workings of this aspect of testing, which occupies more teacher and student time and effort than any other.

Much of the debate on testing over the last two decades has centered on issues of equity. In his cogent and balanced review of testing and the minority child, Leonard Beckum from the Far West Laboratory (San Francisco) explores ways in which we can test and use test results to help all children learn.

One of the major theoretical and practical developments in testing is latent trait research analysis and item response theory. In Chapter Five, Joe Ryan draws on his experience at the University of South Carolina and on his work with the South Carolina State Department of Education to guide practitioners in understanding, evaluating, and using these developments to meet their testing needs.

Microcomputer technology is perhaps the most exciting topic for school people today. In Chapter Six, Ron Hambleton, Ernest Anderson, and Linda Murray review applications of this new technology and provide a helpful road map to the present and future possibilities that the small computer is opening up for testing in the schools.

The last five chapters are case studies that place all the general and theoretical pieces of the testing picture in the context of local and state testing practice. Carol Robinson of Albuquerque, Floraline Stevens and Marilyn Burns of Los Angeles, Cordelia Alexander of Dallas, Glynn Ligon and Kevin

Matter of Austin, and Thomas Saterfiel of Mississippi tell it like it is. By so doing, they help us to ground our hopes and dreams for tomorrow's testing and test use advances on the solid rock of excellent current practice in outstanding local and state school systems.

Walter E. Hathaway
Editor

Walter E. Hathaway is director of research and evaluation Portland, Oregon, public schools.

Foreword

It is probably unusual for the superintendent of an urban American school district to write the foreword for a volume on testing and measurement, but this is an unusual publication. Its subject is testing in the schools, and its chapters have been written by people who work in school districts and for school districts to make testing and measurement a better and more useful tool for decision makers at all levels.

In my present and previous positions as superintendent, I have had the good fortune to encounter different but excellent systems of testing and measurement. From these experiences, I have learned some valuable lessons that I find reflected in the chapters that make up this sourcebook. First, testing and measurement are very powerful tools. They can clarify curriculum expectations, influence community support for schools, shape policy and resource decisions, and, most importantly, help principals and teachers in their work with individual students and parents to help them attain their educational goals. Second, despite the unquestionable usefulness of testing and measurement in our schools, they have only begun to meet their potential. For testing and measurement to do all they can to make schooling more effective and efficient, we need better relationships between local curriculum and testing programs, more thorough preparation of all users of test information in the limits and benefits of test results, better preparation for students in taking tests, concentration on helping teachers to make interim measures of student progress in the intervals between systemwide testing, better ways to ensure equity and fairness in testing and in the use and interpretation of test results, and more extensive exploration and application of such technical advances as those made possible by microprocessors and improvements in measurement methodology.

All these issues and many others are explored in this volume. We are working on such improvements in testing and measurement in our own district. So are many other districts, as the case studies in this volume make clear. I feel that we have much to learn from one another. It is therefore with great pleasure that I commend this issue to the attention of my colleagues in national, state, and local school systems everywhere and to those with whom they work. Quite clearly, our task is to shape testing and measurement into even more powerful instruments for the improvement of learning.

Matthew Prophet

Matthew Prophet is superintendent of the Portland, Oregon, school district.

5

The study of test use in schools by the Center for the Study of Evaluation informs public debate on the uses and abuses of achievement testing.

Uses of Testing in the Schools: A National Profile

Joan L. Herman
Donald W. Dorr-Bremme

Achievement testing is American schools is the subject of widespread and heated policy debate. Critics have decried the arbitrariness of current testing practices (Baker, 1978). They have indicted the validity of tests and attacked them as biased (Perrone, 1978). They have accused testing of narrowing the curriculum, and they have questioned its value for the changing functions of American education (Tyler, 1977). The quality of available tests is also a matter of controversy (Center for the Study of Evaluation, 1979; Huron Institute, 1978), and at least one major teachers' organization has called for a moratorium on the use of standardized tests.

In response to the challenges raised by critics, advocates of testing have asserted that current tests can and do serve a variety of important purposes. Proponents maintain, for example, that testing promotes accountability, facilitates accurate placement and selection decisions, and yields information useful in improving curriculum and instruction.

The project reported in this chapter was performed pursuant to a grant from the National Institute of Education. However, the opinions expressed here do not necessarily reflect the position or policy of the National Institute of Education, and no official endorsement by the National Institute of Education should be inferred.

W. E. Hathaway (Ed.). *Testing in the Schools.* New Directions for Testing and Measurement, no. 19. San Francisco: Jossey-Bass, September 1983.

8

The stakes in the testing debate are high. The nation's investment in school achievement testing is enormous, and both the amount and the variety of testing continue to grow. Given public accountability demands, mandates for minimum competence or proficiency testing, evaluation requirements for federal, state, and local education programs, and a variety of judicial decisions on the responsibilities of public schools, concern over the quality of testing and test use has deepened rapidly. These and other factors have fueled the testing controversy.

Despite the controversy and the important issues that it raises, little information has been forthcoming on the nature of testing as it is actually used in the schools. What functions do tests serve in the classroom? How do teachers and principals use test results? What kinds of tests do principals and teachers trust and rely on most? These and similar questions have gone largely unaddressed. A few studies have indicated teachers' circumspect attitudes toward and limited use of one type of achievement measure, the norm-referenced standardized test (Airasian, 1979; Boyd and others, 1979; Goslin and others, 1965; Resnick, 1981; Salmon-Cox, 1981; Stetz and Beck, 1979). Beyond this, however, the landscape of test uses in American schools has remained largely unexplored.

In this context, a three-year study by the Center for the Study of Evaluation (CSE) at the University of California, Los Angeles, provides basic, new information on classroom achievement testing across the United States. Begun in 1979 (some data analyses are still under way), CSE's research proceeded from broad definitions of *test* and *testing*. It encompassed a wide range of formal assessment measures, such as commercially produced norm- and criterion-referenced tests and curriculum-embedded measures, tests of minimum competence or functional literacy, and district-, school-, and teacher-developed tests. It focused as well on less formal means for gauging student achievement, such as teachers' observations of learners and their interactions with learners. Within this broad field, inquiry focused on achievement assessment practices and uses in reading and English and in mathematics as carried out in public schools at the upper elementary and high school levels. A nationwide survey of teachers and principals was central to the study. Results of this survey form the basis of the report that follows. The research also included interviews with 110 school-level educators (including nine principals and eighty-six teachers) in five school districts across the country. Interview results were consonant with survey findings and afforded researchers a deeper understanding of the latter. While the interview results are not presented here, they have influenced researchers in their interpretation and discussion of survey findings.

In the sections that follow, we describe the survey sample, then report survey findings on two major questions: How important are the results of different types of assessment to teachers' and principals' decisions? What are teachers' and principals' attitudes toward testing? We conclude by drawing the implications of these findings for the public debate on testing and for public policy.

The Survey Sample

The survey addressed a nationwide sample of principals and teachers drawn through a successive random-selection procedure. First, a nationally representative sample of 114 school districts was drawn. Next, districts were stratified on the basis of size, minimum competence testing policy, socioeconomic status, urban–suburban–rural locale, and geographic region. Next, from these districts, size permitting, two elementary schools and two high schools were randomly selected using a procedure that facilitated inclusion of schools at levels serving both higher- and lower-income populations. Finally, at each of these schools, the principal received directions for randomly drawing four teachers for inclusion in the study. The directions for elementary principals specified the random selection of two teachers of tenth-grade English and two teachers of tenth-grade mathematics. At each school, the principal and the four participating teachers received a questionnaire to elicit detailed information on their individual and school testing practices as well as related contextual and attitudinal data.

Returns were obtained from educators in 91 of the 114 districts sampled. Return rates for principals and for teachers at the elementary level approached 60 percent. About 48 percent of the high school teachers responded. To correct for differential return rates by sampling cell and to approximate a nationally representative distribution of respondents, weightings were applied in all analyses. Thus, the results reported here represent our best estimates of national testing practices, test use patterns, and principal and teacher attitudes on testing-related issues.

How Are Test Results Used?

The survey questionnaires sampled a variety of potential purposes of testing and examined the extent to which the results of particular types of tests and other methods of assessment actually serve each purpose. Principals responded about the use of test results for school-level decision making and communication, while teachers reported on classroom uses. The findings are summarized in Tables 1 and 2.

Survey findings indicate that principals consider a wide range of information sources for both decision making and communication. Although no one of these sources is of overpowering importance, it is clear that teachers' opinions and recommendations carry more weight for each of the functions listed than test results do. Of all the purposes that tests serve, required tests—standardized, minimum competence, and tests referenced to district curriculum objectives—seem to contribute most to curriculum evaluation decisions

Table 1. Importance of Test Results for School Decision Making in Elementary and Secondary Schools (Reported by Principals)

[4-point scale: 4 = Crucial Importance – 1 = Unimportant or not used]

ELEMENTARY

Decision Area:	A	B	C	D	E	F
Curriculum Evaluation	3.01 (.67)	2.91 (.75)	3.04 (.87)	2.99	2.94 (.84)	3.27 (.64)
Student Class Assignments	2.50 (.81)	2.35 (.91)	2.46 (.99)	2.44	2.93 (.79)	3.12 (.71)
Teacher Evaluation	1.70 (.76)	1.53 (.78)	1.80 (.93)	1.68	2.12 (.97)	----
Allocating Funds	1.91 (.87)	1.89 (.90)	1.94 (1.01)	1.91	----	3.08 (.71)
Student Promotion	2.65 (.81)	2.31 (.96)	2.38 (.94)	2.45	3.05 (.70)	3.29 (.67)
Public Communication	2.77 (.90)	2.47 (.99)	2.34 (1.00)	2.52	2.31 (1.05)	----
Communicating to Parents	2.91 (.60)	2.64 (.98)	2.67 (.95)	2.74	3.43 (.55)	3.45 (.57)
Reporting to District	3.12 (.68)	2.78 (1.10)	2.74 (1.10)	2.88	2.62 (.91)	----

SECONDARY

	A	B	C	D	E	F
Curriculum Evaluation	2.83 (.67)	3.27 (.64)	2.95 (.82)	3.02	2.76 (.75)	3.14 (.70)
Student Class Assignments	2.77 (.77)	2.98* (.87)	2.78 (.87)	2.84	2.98 (.73)	2.99 (.79)
Teacher Evaluation	1.63 (.74)	1.77 (.71)	1.84 (.78)	1.75	2.39 (.83)	----
Allocating Funds	1.73 (.81)	2.20 (1.13)	2.06 (1.08)	2.00	----	3.34 (.54)
Student Promotion	1.61 (.78)	2.58 (1.28)	2.05 (1.13)	2.08	3.33 (.85)	3.46 (.75)
Public Communication	2.84 (.80)	2.92 (1.03)	2.30 (1.07)	2.69	2.24 (1.05)	----
Communicating to Parents	2.91 (.58)	3.03 (1.00)	2.55 (.99)	2.83	3.56 (.55)	3.38 (.76)
Reporting to District	3.10 (.64)	3.12 (.97)	2.92 (.95)	3.04	2.53 (.88)	----

A = Standardized, norm-referenced test batteries
B = Minimum Competency Tests
C = District Objective-based or Continuum Tests
D = Average Required Tests (A,B,C)
E = Results of Teacher and Curriculum tests
F = Teacher Opinions/Recommendations

Table 2. Importance of Test Results for Teacher Decision Making in Elementary and Secondary Schools (Reported by Teachers)

[4-point scale: 4 = Crucial Importance − 1 = Unimportant or not used]

ELEMENTARY

Decision Area:	A	B	C	D	E
Planning teaching at beginning of the school year	2.53	2.60	----	----	3.39
Initial grouping or placement of students	2.51	2.59	2.91	3.12	3.58
Changing a student from one group or curriculum to another, providing remedial or accelerated work	2.52	2.52	3.04	3.12	3.66
Deciding on report card grades	1.62	1.81	2.89	3.38	3.69

SECONDARY

	A	B	C	D	E
Planning teaching at the beginning of the school year	2.22	2.38	----	----	3.59
Initial grouping or placement of students	2.28	2.46	2.48	3.04	3.84
Changing students from one group or curriculum to another, providing remedial or accelerated work	2.52	2.59	2.67	3.27	3.61
Deciding on report card grades	1.36	1.45	2.29	3.65	3.68

A = Standardized test batteries
B = District Continuum or Minimum Competency Tests
C = Tests Included with Curriculum
D = Teacher-Made Tests
E = Teacher Observations/Opinions

and to communication with parents and school district personnel. However, the same types of tests are least important for teacher evaluations and budget allocations. At the secondary school level, these more formal assessments — particularly minimum competence tests — also play an important role in decisions about student class assignments. Further, while standardized norm-referenced tests seem to be the most influential of the required tests at the elementary school level, minimum competence test results have most significance at the high school level.

Like the principals, teachers were asked to rate the importance of a variety of assessment types for activities with which they are routinely concerned. But, while principals reported on assessment uses for schoolwide activities, teachers were asked about assessment uses in classroom tasks. The results depicted in Table 2 show that both elementary and secondary teachers consider various types of test results to be useful in making a variety of decisions. Clearly, however, teachers accord the highest importance to their own observations of students' work and to their own clinical judgment. For initial grouping or placing of students in a curriculum, for changing students from one group or curriculum to another, and for assigning grades, nearly every teacher reported that his or her own observations and students' classwork were crucial or important sources of information. In addition, the great majority of respondents indicated that the results of tests that they developed themselves also figured as crucial or important in their decisions. Finally, for many elementary school teachers, the results of tests included with the curriculum being used also played an influential role in instructional decision making.

Mirroring the findings for principals, the results for teachers indicate that, while teachers do not attribute heavy importance to the results of required tests, they do view such results as somewhat useful sources of data for initial planning, for initial placement of students in groups or curriculum options, and even for decisions about reassigning students to different instructional groups or curricula throughout the year.

It is apparent from the results of the CSE study that teachers use a variety of sources to make each kind of decision. They do not rely on a single type of information. As one teacher stated, "You can't count a score on one test too heavily. The kid could be sick or tired or just not feel up to doing it that day. Maybe his parents had a fight the night before. Maybe he doesn't try. Maybe he doesn't test well." Moreover, respondents — particularly those at the elementary school level — also reported thinking that many kinds of assesssment techniques give them crucial or important information.

What Are Principals' and Teachers' Attitudes Toward Testing?

Teachers' attitudes toward testing were neither universally negative nor globally positive. Teachers saw testing as a technique that motivates students to study harder (elementary: 73 percent; high school English: 80 percent; high school math: 93 percent), and most teachers agreed that tests of minimum competence should be required of all students for promotion or graduation (elementary: 81 percent; high school English: 86 percent; high school math: 90 percent). Yet, at the same time, teachers expressed substantial concern that minimum competence tests are often unfair to particular students (elementary: 58 percent; high school English: 48 percent; high school mathematics: 35 percent). Moreover, many teachers worried that minimum competence testing would affect the amount of time that they can spend teaching subjects or skills that tests do not cover (elementary: 62 percent; high school English: 62 percent; high school math: 42 percent). Most required tests emphasize the basic skills subjects, and a great majority of the teachers surveyed (elementary: 88 percent; high school English: 84 percent; high school math: 74 percent) felt that basic skills teaching and remedial work are now consuming a substantially increased proportion of school resources.

Teachers appeared to be generally satisfied with the tests that they were required to give. Slightly more than 60 percent of the teachers felt that tests developed in their districts were good. Most elementary teachers (59 percent) but fewer than half of the high school teachers (46 percent in both subject areas) found that the quality of commercial tests is usually high. However, while about three quarters of the teachers perceived that the content and skills tested by most required tests are very similar to the content and skills that they taught, they did not wish to be judged by their students' performance on standardized tests. In contrast to their positive views about minimum competence requirements and student accountability, most teachers agreed that teachers should not be held accountable for students' scores on standardized tests or tests of minimum competence (elementary: 71 percent; high school: 61 percent).

In short, teachers in the CSE survey were certainly not against testing in any general sense. Indeed, high school teachers in particular were very positive about testing. Even more than their elementary school peers, they viewed testing as a motivational tool, and a majority felt that the pressure that testing exerted on schools had had a generally beneficial effect. Other survey results indicate that these attitudes are consistent with testing practices: Compared with elementary school teachers, teachers at the high school level reported spending about twice as much time testing students.

Principals' attitudes toward testing were even more benign. A majority was generally satisfied with the amount of time devoted to required testing and test preparation in their schools. More than half advocated minimum competence test requirements for grade promotion and high school graduation. To a greater extent than teachers, principals perceived that required testing programs resulted in more time being spent in basic skills instruction — English, reading, and math — and they seemed to be comfortable with that shift.

Like teachers, most principals were satisfied with the quality of avail-

14

able tests. More than 80 percent agreed that standardized tests were fair for most students and that the quality of both district-developed tests and commercial curriculum tests was generally good. Almost half, however, expressed concern about the equity of minimum competence tests for some students, and a sizable minority (43 percent) had reservations about the pressure that required testing exerted on them and the teachers at their schools. Nonetheless, most (64 percent) felt that test scores were a fairly good index of how well a school is doing and that schools should be held accountable for students' scores on standardized achievement tests (60 percent) and on minimum competence tests (73 percent). Principals were considerably less comfortable with the idea of using test scores to evaluate teachers, since more than 60 percent of the elementary school principals and about half the secondary principals asserted that test scores should not be used to evaluate teachers' effectiveness or competence.

Summary and Conclusions

We began this discussion by noting the public controversy over the quality and usefulness of testing. In concluding, it is worth asking whether the results of the CSE national survey indicate that testing is controversial among educators in our schools. The answer is yes. When we review the attitude data reported in the preceding section, we realize that the majority of teachers and certainly the majority of principals are in generally positive about testing. Most think highly of the quality of most available tests, both those produced commercially and those developed in house. Most educators think that testing helps motivate students to study harder. Most advocate testing requirements for high school graduation. Furthermore, many teachers and principals rate all types of test results to which they have access as at least somewhat important and quite often as important or critical in carrying out their routine professional tasks.

At the same time, however, substantial minorities of teachers—often on the order of 30 to 40 percent—express critical views of testing. These teachers are not satisfied with the quality of available tests. Moreover, high proportions of teachers are concerned about the fairness of minimum competence tests and the tendency of such testing programs to narrow the curriculum. (In on-site interviews, teachers elaborated on these same concerns.) In the preceding sections, we emphasized general trends in the data: mean ratings and majority choices. But these trends should not obscure the fact that substantial numbers of teachers (and, to a lesser extent, of principals) seem to be genuinely concerned about the quality and uses of testing in contemporary American schooling. In short, there does appear to be some marked disagreement among school-level educators about achievement testing issues. The validity and significance of the public controversy about testing appears to be confirmed by our survey.

The survey also confirms the validity of some concerns about the impact of required testing on schools. While concerns about inappropriate use or mis-use of tests do not appear to be well founded, the data do indicate that the very presence of required testing has significant consequences on education. School personnel agree that more time is spent in teaching basic skills — English, language arts, and mathematics — as a result of required testing and that less attention can be paid to other subject areas as a result. Admittedly, tests alone have not caused the curriculum to narrow. Rather, the narrowing is a consequence of the importance ascribed by society at large to test scores and of an emphasis on basic skills. Nonetheless, it might be well both for the public and for policy makers to consider whether the limited sample of skills assessed by most standardized tests represents an adequate curriculum and whether test developers, rather than teachers, administrators, and the community, ought to be defining the curriculum.

What else does the CSE research have to tell us? First, the survey suggests that those in the education and testing communities have paid far too little attention to the matter of teachers' assessment skills. For the most part, the debate on testing has been played out in exchanges about the relative merits of normed and criterion-referenced measures, in discussion of cultural and linguistic biases in standardized tests, in sociopolitical controversy over proficiency testing, and so on. It has focused on measures employed nationwide or statewide that generally have been developed by commercial testing concerns or by other large agencies that employ psychometricians. It is appropriate for us to be concerned about the qualities and social implications of such tests. Although they figure less heavily in principals' and teachers' decisions and they consume only small proportions of classroom time, tests of this type figure (often as the only consideration) in major educational gate-keeping decisions. However, the quality of teachers' assessment skills — their skills as test developers and as clinical classroom diagnosticians — have largely escaped attention. Yet the cumulative record of teacher-made tests, the grades in which they result, as well as the teachers' informal judgments of children's competence clearly influence students' educational careers and life chances in major ways, perhaps to a degree exceeding that of more formal testing. What is more, students — particularly secondary students — spend large proportions of their testing time taking teacher-developed and teacher-scheduled tests.

We know very little about the quality of the teacher-developed tests. We do know that few states explicitly require competence in test development and test selection for teacher certification. Ebel (1967) identified common errors in teacher-constructed tests and urged better training in this area. More recent research indicates that teachers remain poorly prepared in assessment (Rudman and others, 1980; Yeh and others, 1981). Preservice training and certification requirements demand virtually nothing in formal course work in testing (Woellner, 1979), and in-service training does little to fill the gap. Only about one fifth of the teachers in our survey received in-service experiences related to selection and construction of good tests or in use of test results to improve instruction. Clearly, teachers need training opportunities if they are to be competent test developers and literate consumers of test information.

In summary, it seems worth considering just how qualified today's teachers are to be developers of the tests that most affect students' lives. How effective are teacher-generated tests in revealing the insufficiencies in individual students' learning? How valid are they as measures of students' achievement? How do teachers decide how often to test? How skilled are elementary school teachers in analyzing the commercial curriculum-embedded tests that they frequently use? Similar questions can also be raised about teachers' skills in making observation- and interaction-based judgments of children's learning.

Given the time spent on teacher-constructed tests and given the cumulative importance both of these tests and of teachers' judgments in classroom and schoolwide decision making, teachers' preparation for the role of achievement assessor and their competence in that role need thorough review. And this review deserves the attention of both the educational policy and the educational testing communities.

While we work to improve the quality of teacher-made tests, we must also strive to improve the usefulness of more formal measures. Our research suggests three general but highly important qualities that the more formal measures should have, qualities that are inherent in the teacher-developed and curriculum-embedded tests that teachers use most frequently: a close match to curriculum, immediate availability and accessibility, and personal ownership. That is, formal measures must reflect what is being taught in class, and they must be sensitive to teachers' intentions and emphases as teachers themselves perceive them. Moreover, teachers must be able to administer these measures to students when they feel it appropriate, and the results must be both understandable and available promptly. Finally, the content, format, and timing of the measures must be under the control and discretion of individual teachers. Many commercial, state, district, and school testing programs do not have these characteristics, and the results are predictable: a system that is of little use to teachers and that teachers little use. The formal sytems may surpass teacher products in sophistication and technical quality, but little benefit accrues if they are not fully used.

Our research shows that there are two major paths to improvements in the quality and usefulness of the measurement of student achievement. Universities, state and local policy makers and administrators, test developers, and teachers must walk these paths together if educators are to make better decisions to help students learn.

References

Airasian, P. W. "The Effects of Standardized Testing and Test Information on Teachers' Perceptions and Practices." Paper presented at the annual meeting of the American Educational Research Association, San Francisco, 1979.

17

Baker, E. L. "Is Something Better Than Nothing? Metaphysical Test Design." Paper presented at the 1978 CSE Measurement and Methodology Conference, Los Angeles, 1978.

Boyd, J., Jacobsen, K., McKenna, B. H., Stake, R. E., and Yashinsky, J. *A Study of Testing Practices in the Royal Oak (Michigan) Public Schools.* Royal Oak: Royal Oak Michigan School District, 1975.

Center for the Study of Evaluation. *CSE Criterion-Referenced Test Handbook.* Los Angeles, Calif.: Center for the Study of Evaluation, 1979.

Ebel, R. L. "Improving the Competence of Teachers in Educational Measurement." In J. Flynn and H. Garber (Eds.), *Assessing Behavior: Readings in Educational and Psychological Measurement.* Reading, Mass.: Addison-Wesley, 1967.

Goslin, D. A., Epstein, R., and Hilloch, B. A. *The Use of Standardized Tests in Elementary Schools.* Second Technical Report. New York: Russell Sage Foundation, 1965.

Huron Institute. *Summary of the Spring Conference of the National Consortium on Testing.* Cambridge, Mass.: Huron Institute, 1978.

Perrone, V. "Remarks to the National Conference on Achievement Testing and Basic Skills." Paper presented at the National Conference on Achievement Testing and Basic Skills, Washington, D.C., March 1978.

Resnick, L. B. "Introduction: Research to Inform a Debate." *Phi Delta Kappan,* 1981, *62* (9), 623–624.

Rudman, H. C., Kelly, J. L., Wanous, D. S., Mehrens, W. A., Clark, C. M., and Porter, A. C. *Integrating Assessment with Instruction: A Review 1922–1980.* East Lansing, Mich.: Institute for Research on Teaching, 1980.

Salmon-Cox, L. "Teachers and Tests: What's Really Happening?" *Phi Delta Kappan,* 1981, *62* (9), 631–634.

Stetz, F., and Beck, M. "Teachers' Opinions of Standardized Test Use and Usefulness." Paper presented at the annual meeting of the American Educational Research Association, San Francisco, 1979.

Tyler, R. "What's Wrong with Standardized Testing." *Today's Education,* 1977, *66* (2), 35–38.

Woellner, R. S. "Let's Use Tests for Teaching: Standardized Test Results Can Provide the Basis for a Program of Instruction." *Teacher,* 1979, *90* (2), 62–64, 179–181.

Yeh, J. P., Herman, J. L., and Rudner, L. M. *Teachers and Testing: A Survey of Test Use.* Report No. 166. Los Angeles: Center for the Study of Evaluation, 1981.

Joan L. Herman is assistant director of the Center for the Study of Evaluation, University of California–Los Angeles.

Donald W. Dorr-Bremme is a senior research associate at the Center for the Study of Evaluation and director of the test use project.

Do we sacrifice valuable instructional time to teach testwiseness
strategies at the last minute before a standardized test?
Year-long preparation involving teachers and parents
appears to be the better alternative.

Preparing Students for Standardized Testing

Glynn D. Ligon

Why do teachers and principals feel such a strong need to prepare students for standardized testing above and beyond the regular classroom instruction that has been provided? In most cases, this compulsion arises not from lack of confidence in their teaching ability but rather from a concern that test scores will not adequately reflect students' true skills levels. Less frequently, there is a desire to raise test scores as high as possible. Whatever its source, the national trend toward making students testwise has led some teachers and principals to arm students with strategies for outguessing the testmakers and answering items whose correct answers they do not know. The result is less accurate rather than more accurate measurement.

Why Do Students Score Low?

For educators to prepare students to do their best on standardized tests, we must first know what factors inhibit optimal performance. If teachers nationwide were polled to discover the most common causes of poor performance on standardized tests, they would probably list the same eight reasons cited by Austin, Texas, teachers: test anxiety—being so concerned about scores that students function below their true ability levels; carelessness—being undermotivated or having poor test-taking skills; confusion—being over-

W. E. Hathaway (Ed.). *Testing in the Schools*. New Directions for Testing
and Measurement, no. 19. San Francisco: Jossey-Bass, September 1983.

whelmed by unfamiliar procedures and item formats; poor use of time—being too meticulous, not using time to recheck answers, and so forth; unsuccessful guessing—being unable to guess the correct answer; lack of skills—being too far below grade level to have the skills required to answer a reasonable number of test items correctly; special circumstances—being hindered in taking the test by unusual circumstances, such as illness, noise from outside the classroom, or a defective test booklet; and handicapping conditions—being so physically, mentally, or emotionally handicapped that a valid test score is unlikely.

The first four reasons—test anxiety, carelessnesss, confusion, and poor use of time—are the legitimate targets of preparation activities. The fifth reason—unsuccessful guessing—is controversial; I do not think that attempts to address it represent a productive investment of instructional time. The last three reasons—lack of skills, special circumstances, and handicapping conditions—are long-range issues and require attention that goes beyond that preparation for testing.

Test anxiety can be a symptom of a more serious problem, and referral for counseling can be the best approach for a few students. However, mild anxiety serves to put most students at their competitive peak. Poor past test performance and high expectations by either the student or by another person for the student can contribute to test anxiety. Fear of the unknown or the unfamiliar can be an underestimated factor. Unfamiliar directions, item formats, vocabulary, and time constraints can all prevent a student from recognizing or responding with answers that the student knows. Add to these the heightened atmosphere created when desks are pushed away from each other and when the whole school is synchronized for directions and breaks. Top it all off with test items more difficult than those encountered on teacher-made tests.

Possibly the most frustrating factor for teachers is students' carelessness. Carelessness can be attributed to low motivation, failure to keep one's place, or failure to attend to the most relevant details of an item. Unfamiliarity with a test's format and directions can be interpreted as carelessness when confusion is the real culprit. That is, confusion about test directions, item formats, and other test procedures can cost students time and contribute to their test anxiety and their seeming carelessness. Finally, many students do not know how to use time in the most productive manner. Indeed, some students encounter restrictive time limits for the first time or for the only time during the school year when they take a standardized test.

Fortunately, all four problems can be addressed in simple classroom experiences prior to testing. The unfamiliarity of the testing situation is the common denominator of all four problems. Thus, the best solution is to give students prior experience with the features of standardized tests that are uncharacteristic of regular classroom instruction and teacher-made tests: multiple-choice items, the wide variety of item formats, time limits, separate answer sheets, circles that the student must bubble in, and more difficult items.

A Philosophy for Preparing Students for Standardized Testing

The competing claims of teaching the test, teaching to the test, and encouraging guessing through testwiseness strategies usually attract the most attention when educators discuss preparing students for standardized tests. However, the real issues should be these: How can we get the most valid and reliable measure of each student's skills, and how much instructional time should we sacrifice to test preparation? Consider the following two-part philosophy for preparing students for standardized testing: An appropriate activity for preparing students for standardized testing is "one which contributes to students' performing on the test near their true achievement levels, and one which contributes more to their scores than would an equal amount of regular classroom instruction" (Ligon and Jones, 1982, p. 1). With this philosophy, teaching the test, teaching to the test, and encouraging guessing through test-wiseness strategies can all be inappropriate if they inflate students' scores above true achievement levels or if they divert time from valuable basic skills instruction. This is the philosophy that Austin's public schools have adopted. To believe that all eighty-two schools have embraced the philosophy would be foolish. However, the Austin school system now has a rational, defensible criterion for judging the merits of preparation activities.

A Year-Long Plan of Action

What good is a philosophy without a plan of action? The plan that is most appropriate to this two-part philosophy is one that is very protective of instructional time. Therefore, the key lies in using regular classroom activities as the vehicles for preparing students for standardized testing. In this way, instructional time can be conserved, and students do not perceive the standardized test as a trial in preparation for which everything else must be put aside for two weeks.

The real burden in this effort naturally falls on classroom teachers. Teacher-made tests and classwork designed to incorporate the six features of standardized tests listed two sections ago can provide experiences and practice similar to those acquired by taking a standardized test. The ultimate objective is to have students be familiar with the situation when they sit down to take a standardized test. That will reduce their confusion and their test anxiety. In the Austin public schools, preparation of students for standardized testing is year-long. While there are special activities, such as informative talks and practice tests, one or two days prior to testing, teachers are encouraged to incorporate the six features into their lessons and tests all year long.

Teachers have been most concerned about the confusing, busy, crowded nature of standardized tests. Apparently, publishers need to save paper, because they pack as many items as they can onto a single page. Add to this item formats that teachers do not naturally use on their own tests. If teachers used the item and page formats of standardized tests in their classwork and on their own tests, they could be criticized for teaching to the test. Therefore, teachers should use as wide a variety of formats as possible in all their students' work. They should give students experience with many different layouts and item structures. Then, when students encounter a relatively unfamiliar format on a standardized test, they will react to it as just another way of asking the same question.

Timing seatwork activity—asking all students to start and stop at the same time—is almost unheard of in classrooms. However, this is a type of experience that students need. At the end of one school year, the parents of two students, not in the same family, called our testing office to ask why their children's standardized test scores were lower than their classroom performance had led the parents to expect. In both cases, the answer was the same. Neither child had been required during the year to work within time constraints. Their answer sheet patterns were similar: A very high percentage of the answers marked were correct, but neither student finished the test. This problem cannot be remedied in the time just prior to testing. Effective time-use habits can be learned through year-long experience much better than through a pretest lecture about skipping difficult items and going back to them later.

In Austin, multiple-choice items are not a unique experience for students taking standardized tests. In fact, as teachers discover the time that can be saved by multiple-choice items compared to open-ended or essay items, we can begin to worry that too large a proportion of students' test questions during the school year will be multiple choice. Although we must encourage teachers to incorporate multiple-choice items and separate answer sheets with circles that students bubble in to indicate their choices, we must also encourage them to continue to use open-ended and essay exercises. After all, one of the shortcomings of standardized tests is that they exclude composition skills and creative thinking.

A Review of the Literature on Test Preparation

Much research was reviewed, and some research was conducted before the Austin test preparation philosophy and program were developed (Jones and Ligon, 1982). The literature identifies three categories of student preparation activities: testwiseness, test practice, and practice tests.

Testwiseness. The most common definition of testwiseness is "a subject's capacity to utilize the characteristics and formats of the test and/or the test-taking situation to receive a high score. Testwiseness is logically independent of the examinee's knowledge of the subject matter for which the items are supposedly measures" (Millman and others, 1965, p. 707). Testwiseness affects scores on standardized tests, and the differences in scores caused by testwiseness become error; that is, they are not due to differences in the trait that the tests seek to measure. The construct of testwiseness is well documented in the psychometric literature. Slakter and others (1970a; 1970b), Diamond and Evans (1972), and Flynn and Anderson (1977) have all devised instruments to measure testwiseness. In summarizing the research literature, Jongsma and Warshauer (1975, p. 18) concluded that "testwiseness can be effectively taught to students of all ages from preschool through adult. Although the results have not always been statistically significant, the gains nearly always favor the instructional group."

At this point, it will be helpful to distinguish between two types of testwiseness skills. First, basic testwiseness skills include marking answers properly, using available time efficiently, and following directions. Basic testwiseness skills help to reduce the error in test scores. Second, advanced testwiseness skills include choosing the grammatically correct alternative and avoiding options with *always* and *never*. Advanced skills should seldom be advantageous to students on a well-constructed standardized test. Thus, the chances of reducing student errors on a major standardized test by teaching advanced testwiseness skills appear to be small.

When the benefits of ten advanced testwiseness strategies were studied using the Iowa Tests of Basic Skills, Reading Comprehension Tests, Levels 9–12 (Ligon and Jones, 1982), the benefits were far from impressive. Two strategies were found to be useful: Using the content of other items and eliminating outrageous, illogical, or vague options. Both strategies are acceptable to the philosophy outlined earlier, because they require students to use partial or available knowledge to determine the correct answer. The effects of using seven other strategies were also studied: choosing the noticeably longer option, choosing the more carefully worded option, choosing the option with the most specific details, eliminating options with specific determiners, looking for a resemblance between option and stem, inferring the intent of the test maker, and looking for a grammatical consistency between option and stem. These strategies were useful for very few items, and they were deemed to be inappropriate for teaching to students for four reasons. First, all these strategies rely on cues that are not specific to the skill being mastered. Second, the skill required to apply the strategy correctly is often more difficult than the skill that the item measures. Third, several factors lower the chances that these strategies will actually help on a meaningful number of items: The student has to choose correctly from among several strategies on some items; pure guessing provides correct answers in one out of four or five instances; and on about half the items, it is likely that the average student already knows the answer. Fourth, testwiseness strategies are virtually useless in a number of important areas, including math, spelling, punctuation, and capitalization.

Practice Tests. A distinction needs to be made between the terms *practice test* and *test practice*. The term *practice test* refers to exercises for students, designed by testmakers or school personnel, much shorter in length and typically much easier than the standardized tests to which they relate. Practice tests are usually designed to familiarize students with the visual format of a test and with the terminology used in test instructions, provide students with practice in using separate answer sheets, and to ease students' fear of the test. There has been little research on the effects of practice tests on test scores and on the reliability or predictive power of practice tests. Teachers consistently report that easy practice tests fail to prepare students for the longer and much more difficult standardized test.

Test Practice. The term *test practice* refers to the use of full-length standardized tests as practice prior to the administration of a standardized test for official purposes. Especially where intelligence and aptitude tests are concerned, there is ample research on the effects of test practice on test scores. The findings regarding intelligence tests are remarkably consistent. Peel (1952), Kreit (1968), and Eichelberger (1971) have found that only one test practice session within one month of the actual test can improve IQ scores. Any further test practice is useless, all three researchers conclude, because a second or third practice session does not affect IQ scores, regardless of the time interval between test practice and the official test. If the interval is more than two months, the official test scores probably will be unaffected by test practice. Using an aptitude battery, Nero (1976) found that practice effects lingered for as long as ten months if the posttest was either the same as the pretest or a parallel form. Nero's study further shows that improved performance based on test practice results not from repetition (at least at ten-month intervals) but from subjects' familiarity with the test's format.

Who Must Be Prepared?

Students are not the only ones who must be prepared. Teachers and parents must also be prepared. Experience shows that teachers' perceptions of standardized tests often influence their attitudes toward preparing students to be tested. Obviously, a teacher who has a negative attitude toward tests can pass that attitude on to students. However, there are also some misperceptions that must be remedied.

Some teachers believe that standardized tests are too difficult for low achievers. Strictly speaking, this belief is not a misperception but the result of a misperception. Standardized tests are designed so that the average student can answer slightly more than half the items correctly. In contrast, teacher-made tests are designed to yield an average score that can be converted into the grade of C. In fact, elementary teachers in Austin reported that they expected their average student to answer about 75 percent of the items on teacher-made tests correctly. This compares to an average (fiftieth percentile) score on the Iowa Tests of Basic Skills of 57 percent of the items correct (Ligon and Jones, 1982). Standardized tests are more difficult. However, students' scores on standardized tests are converted into percentiles and grade equivalents, which tend to match teachers' perceptions of their students' skills fairly closely. This is the point that teachers need to consider. The more difficult items on standardized tests will not necessarily result in an invalidly low test score for average and below-average students.

Teachers tend also to underestimate the ability that students will demonstrate on standardized tests. Here, we are talking not about underestimating students' percentile ranks but about underestimating how well students will handle confusing formats, separate answer sheets, and complex wordings. Historically, when Austin teachers have reviewed standardized tests, they have judged the tests to be more difficult for children to take than the children's performance reveals them to be. For example, teachers insist that students below grade four cannot handle separate answer sheets and that they should be allowed to mark in the test booklet. However, a pilot test showed that third graders who had no prior experience of marking answers on a computer bubble sheet could do so with ease. In fact, after processing thousands of answer sheets in the past few years, our systemwide testing staff concur that third graders bubble in answers more dextrously and neatly than junior high students do.

The bottom line for teachers is that standardized tests are more difficult than teacher-made tests. But, rather than being interpreted in the usual test-score-to-letter-grade manner, the raw scores are converted into percentiles and grade equivalents. In addition, students appear to handle standardized tests better than most teachers seem to expect. Thus, we need to select our areas of concern carefully to avoid overreacting to a perceived problem.

Parents also have a role in preparing students for standardized testing. Parents can help to establish the proper context for testing. As it is for teachers, the role of parent is not a last-minute event but an ongoing series of activities. Educators must communicate to parents that they should follow nine steps each year: know when testing is scheduled and what tests or what types of tests are being give. The parent should show an interest in testing by talking to the child about when the testing will take place, what the teacher has said about the testing, and whether the child needs anything for the test, such as pencils and erasers. Parents should emphasize to children that they must try to do their best so the results will be as accurate as possible. Parents should be supportive. They should communicate that the test is important, but they should urge the children not to worry about it. They should avoid using rewards or sanctions as motivators.

On testing days the parents should avoid events that might upset the child, be sure that the child gets a good night's sleep, prepare a good breakfast, and be sure that the child gets to school on time. After the test, the parent should ask how everything went. The parent should tell the child that the tests are important and that trying to do one's best is a good sign of growing up. The parent should look for the results. When they arrive, the parent should discuss them with the child, looking for areas that the child can be proud of and for areas where the child needs to improve. Parents should avoid comparing their own child with other children and use only the child's own past test

26

scores when comparisons are made. Finally, the parent should attend a parent-teacher conference.

Public service announcements on radio and television are an effective way of providing parents with needed information. They are very time restrictive—between ten and thirty seconds on the average—so only brief messages can be communicated. However, use of well-known people, such as a governor, mayor, or sports personality, to deliver the message can add credence to the message. The message may contain only the suggestion that students should get a good night's sleep, eat a good breakfast, and be at school on time, but raising the awareness level of parents and students about testing is the main purpose.

Standardized Preparation Activities: A School System Necessity

Any school system that compares the achievement test scores of groups of students for any purpose must face the issue of standardizing the preparation that students receive prior to testing. The literature is clear that preparation activities can make a difference. Thus, an educator, evaluator, or researcher who intends to make comparisons must also consider the type and style of preparation activities in which students participate. The speculations that the national norming sample received a minimum of preparation prior to testing is of note in this regard.

For Austin's eighty-two public schools, we have addressed this issue by specifying the preparation activities that must be provided, the activities that must not be provided, and the activities that may be provided. These specifications, which are consistent with the philosophy detailed earlier, are intended not to mandate how each child will be prepared but to restrict the range of preparation that occurs across schools. Most principals and teachers seem to appreciate having the guidelines as a way of ensuring that their students will be as well prepared as the students on other campuses.

Conclusion

Preparation of students for standardized testing should span more than the week just before testing, and it should involve the teacher and the parent as well as the student. The challenge in preparing students for testing is to make the testing important enough that students are motivated to do well but not so important that the test is overemphasized or that regular instruction is sacrificed.

References

Diamond, J., and Evans, W. "An Investigation of the Cognitive Correlates of Test-wiseness." *Journal of Educational Measurement*, 1972, *9*, 145–150.
Eichelberger, R. T. "Practice Effects of Repeated IQ Testing and the Relationship Between IQ Change Scores and Selected Individual Characteristics." *Dissertation Abstracts International*, 1971, *31*, 5196A.

Flynn, J. T., and Anderson, D. E. "The Effects of Test Item Cue Sensitivity on IQ and Achievement Test Performance." *Educational Research Quarterly*, 1977, *2*, 32–39.

Jones, P., and Ligon, G. D. "Preparing Students for Standardized Testing: A Literature Review." Paper presented at the annual meeting of the American Educational Research Association, New York, April 1982.

Jongsma, E. A., and Warshauer, E. "The Effects of Instruction in Test-Taking Skills upon Student Performance on Standardized Achievement Tests." New Orleans: New Orleans University, 1975. (ERIC document ED 114 408)

Kreit, L. H. "The Effects of Practice on the Acquisition of Test-Taking Skills by a Selected Group of Third-Grade Pupils." *Dissertation Abstracts International*, 1968, *28*, 3511A.

Ligon, G. D., and Jones, P. "Preparing Students for Standardized Testing: One District's Perspective." Paper presented at the annual meeting of the American Research Association, New York, April 1982.

Millman, J., Bishop, C. H., and Ebel, R. "An Analysis of Testwiseness." *Educational and Psychological Measurement*, 1965, *25*, 707–726.

Nero, B. "The Effects of General Practice, Specific Practice, and Item Familiarization on Change in Aptitude Test Scores." *Measurement and Evaluation in Guidance*, 1976, *9*, 16–20.

Peel, E. A. "Practice Effects Between Three Consecutive Tests of Intelligence." *British Journal of Educational Psychology*, 1952, *22*, 196–199.

Slakter, M. J., Koehler, R. A., and Hampton, S. H. "Learning Testwiseness by Programmed Texts." *Journal of Educational Measurement*, 1970a, *7*, 247–254.

Slakter, M. J., Koehler, R. A., and Hampton, S. H. "Grade Level, Sex, and Selected Aspects of Testwiseness." *Journal of Educational Measurement*, 1970b, *7*, 119–122.

Glynn D. Ligon is senior evaluator for Austin's systemwide achievement and minimum competency testing programs. Since 1979, he has headed the effort to improve the validity and usefulness of achievement test scores.

The view through the windows shows an essay void and classroom tests that require remembering, rather than use of knowledge.

Teacher-Made Tests: Windows on the Classroom

Margaret Fleming
Barbara Chambers

Teacher-made tests for the purpose of judging students' learning are a common occurrence in the classroom. At every level, kindergarten to university, teachers develop a variety of classroom tests tailored to their particular teaching objectives; these measures are used at various transition points in their instruction. Recent reviews of the literature on teachers' use of tests substantiate the crucial role of teacher-made paper-and-pencil instruments in providing teachers with information about students (Yeh, 1980). These reviews also underscore the need for broad-based information on the nature and use of teacher-made tests (Lazar-Morrison and others, 1980). During the past decade, the continuing controversy about standardized tests diverted attention from concerns about how well teachers used "home-grown" assessment strategies, particularly teacher-made paper-and-pencil tests, in their classrooms. It has even been suggested that teacher-made tests can remedy problems associated with standardized tests (Quinto and McKenna, 1977). Yet, little is known about the nature of teacher-made tests as teachers use them.

The instrument utilized in this study has been revised and expanded by the authors from a rating instrument appearing in Chambers, B. A., "Development and Evaluation of a Teacher-Training Package Designed to Increase Science Teachers' Classroom Test Skills." Unpublished doctoral dissertation, University of Maryland, 1979.

W. E. Hathaway (Ed.). *Testing in the Schools.* New Directions for Testing and Measurement, no. 19. San Francisco: Jossey-Bass, September 1983.

29

This chapter uses teacher-made tests as windows on the classroom through which we can gaze to learn both how teachers test and what they teach. It describes a review procedure and an analytical process used by the Cleveland school district to determine the technical merits as well as cognitive levels in teacher-made tests. It also discusses how teachers can improve their test-making skills and raise the cognitive levels of learning outcomes.

The Technical Review

When a federal court order for desegregation of the Cleveland school district required all tests, including teacher-made tests, to be developed, administered, scored, and used in a nondiscriminatory manner, systematic technical analyses of teacher-made tests became a mandate for the school district. While the need to study teachers' actual testing practices had long been recognized, the court order provided the necessary momentum for addressing that long-standing need.

To achieve compliance with the court order, the school district designed and implemented a periodic quality control check of teacher-made tests across all grade levels in all schools. Now in its third year of implementation, the plan includes maintenance of a test file in each school and establishment of a review cycle by grade and subject for periodic rating of a random sample of tests in a particular area. Review teams composed of administrators, supervisors, and teachers use a locally designed instrument to determine the strengths and weaknesses of individual tests. Different teams review tests from each subject area.

The instrument used to evaluate the technical properties of teacher-made tests is based on one developed by Chambers and Fleming (1982) from an original version designed by Chambers. The first section focuses on the test document itself. It asks reviewers to weigh the arrangement of test questions, the numbering system, the format, the directions, the assignment of point values, and the legibility of individual copies in keeping with recommended standards for production of test documents. The first section also includes a review of the test questions' freedom from bias, as required by the district's court mandate. The review process involves examining the language of test questions for universal and nondiscriminatory attitudes or for ethnic, racial, or sexual bias. For the ten characteristics in this first section of the rating instrument, each rater checks *yes, no, cannot be determined,* or *not applicable.*

The second section contains a checklist that judges the quality of test questions by item type: multiple-choice, true-false, matching, short-answer response (completion), and essay. For each item type, four or five characteristics of sound items are listed. Before the rating team uses the test item checklist, it assigns each item on the test being rated to one of the five categories. For example, the category of short-answer response includes questions that direct students to fill in blanks; to write responses to direct questions; to supply words, numbers, or both in response to numerical problems; to identify pictures; to label diagrams; to write definitions; and to translate words, sentences, or both. For the test being rated, the review team indicates whether all items, most items, or no items fit the characteristics listed for each item type. The options *cannot be determined* and *not applicable* are also provided.

The third part of the rating instrument is an open-ended general comments section. Raters are encouraged to offer suggestions for improvement, to commend quality tests, or to explain the ratings assigned. Reviewers are also encouraged to add observations based on their role in the review team either as a test technician or as a subject matter specialist. Reviewers have provided constructive recommendations. They have suggested how the congruence of test items to intended course outcomes in the district's courses of study can be improved, and they have recommended redesign of test items to reflect sound measurement principles. Reviewers also are interested in identifying creative test approaches and in providing support to teachers who take imaginative approaches in designing classroom tests. To make the test review process as reliable as possible, review team members take part in orientation activities in which they apply the rating instrument to a sample test.

The Content Review

As the review process generated information about technical aspects of 342 teacher-made tests in twelve grade and subject areas reviewed over a two-year period, it became apparent that further analyses of the 8,800 test questions contained in the tests could provide new insights about the aspects of pupil behavior that teachers valued enough to test. Many authors (Bloom and others, 1981; Ebel, 1979; Gronlund, 1976; Hills, 1981) say that development of appropriate specifications for teacher-made classroom tests involves definition not only of content areas for all test questions but behavioral categories as well. For this reason, the second state of the review process that we implemented in Cleveland classified test questions according to behavioral categories—what Ebel (1979), p. 83) terms "overt item characteristics." In that review, we used the six behavioral categories delineated by Bloom and others (1981): knowledge of terms, knowledge of facts, knowledge of rules and principles, skill in using processes and procedures, ability to make translations, and ability to make applications.

Recognizing that explanation and some practice in applying these categories would be required, Bloom and others (1981) reported that agreement between judges could be achieved in 85 percent or more of the classifications in their categories through explanation and practice. Bloom's experience proved true in our effort. Most of the doubts arose in making distinctions between facts and rules or principles and between translations and applications. In the first instance, the decision rested on whether the test question referred to a particular fact or principle in the directions or stem. In the second instance, test questions that required students to solve problems, to recognize or identify essentials in problems, or to choose relevant rules or principles as a basis for problem solution before solving the problem were classified as requiring application behaviors. Questions that directed students to transform material from one form into another, such as from verbal into numerical or symbolic form, or to put ideas into their own words were classified as translations. Application behaviors proved to be the most complex of all, typically depending on behaviors represented by other categories but requiring students to apply these behaviors in new problems.

Opening the Windows

Table 1 provides a tally of samples of teacher-made tests rated by grade and subject and classified by item type and levels of pupil behaviors. The tests included in our analyses represented all major academic subjects and all grade levels. Table 1 lists the average number of test questions for each test sample and the percentages of item types and pupil behaviors represented by the test questions reviewed.

How Do Teachers Test?

Eight observations about how teachers test in the Cleveland school district emerge from study of Table 1: First, teachers use short-answer questions most frequently in their test making. Second, teachers, even English teachers, generally avoid essay questions, which represent slightly more than 1 percent of all test items reviewed. Third, teachers use more matching items than multiple-choice or true-false items. Fourth, teachers devise more test questions to sample knowledge of facts than any of the other behavioral categories studied. Fifth, when categories related to knowledge of terms, knowledge of facts, and knowledge of rules and principles are combined, almost 80 percent of the test questions reviewed focus on these areas. Sixth, teachers develop few questions to test behaviors that can be classified as ability to make applications. Seventh, comparison across school levels shows that junior high school teachers use more questions to tap knowledge of terms, knowledge of facts, and knowledge of rules and principles than elementary or senior high school teachers do. Almost 94 percent of their questions address knowledge categories, contrasted with 69 percent of the senior high school teachers' questions and 69 percent of the elementary school teachers' questions. Finally, at all grade levels, teacher-made mathematics and science tests reflect a diversity of behavioral categories, since they typically feature questions in all six behavioral categories.

Test directions and statements of point values for test questions were noticeably absent from the test samples. Less than two thirds of all the tests reviewed included directions for each item type, while less than 12 percent of all tests included point values. Teachers generally grouped all test questions by

Table 1. Summary of Percentages of Ratings of Teacher-Made Tests[1]

Type of School	Subject	Grade Levels	No. of Tests in Sample	Avg. No. of Items in Test	Percentages of Item Types					Percentages of Levels of Behavior						Total No. of Items
					M.C.	T.F.	Match.	S.A.R.	Esy.	Terms	Facts	Rules, Princ.	Proc., Prod.	Trans.	Applic.	
Elementary	Language Arts	1-3	42	15	0	0	0	100	0	2	4	80	0	13	0	623
	Language Arts	4-6	31	21	7	1	10	82	0	10	1	73	12	4	0	651
	Mathematics	4-6	45	24	4	2	5	89	0	5	2	25	41	10	18	1059
	Soc. Studies	1-6	49	17	11	21	28	38	2	21	73	0	0	6	1	843
Total Elementary Tests			167	19	6	6	11	77	-[2]	9	21	39	14	10	7	3176
Junior High	English	7-9	27	37	7	8	22	62	2	25	42	32	0	1	0	1000
	Industrial Arts	7-9	30	23	19	13	5	61	2	17	57	20	6	0	0	675
	Science	7-9	24	33	35	16	29	19	1	29	20	36	1	12	2	802
	Social Studies	7-9	23	44	15	19	38	25	3	10	89	0	0	1	0[2]	1006
Total Junior High Tests			104	33	18	14	25	41	2	20	53	21	1	3	2	3483
Senior High	English	10-12	17	32	23	15	35	25	2	21	71	4	4	0	0	542
	French	10-12	12	35	21	0	4	74	1	17	4	23	0	55	1	422
	Mathematics	10-12	20	34	0	0	11	89	0	7	8	15	44	21	5	454
	Science	10-12	22	23	33	10	30	26	1	28	45	16	4	5	2	742
Total Senior High Tests			71	30	21	7	22	49	1	19	36	14	11	18	2	2160
Total All Grades		1-12	342	26	14	10	19	56	1	16	38	26	8	9	3	8819

[1] Percentages are rounded.
[2] Less than 1%.

question type and used the same format for presenting test questions of a particular type. Teachers' numbering systems depended on the type of test questions, but about one half of the tests for elementary grades had no numbered test items. Although junior and senior high school teachers were more inclined to number tests questions, their tendency was to divide tests, especially long tests, into sections tagged either with roman numerals or with letters in alphabetical order. These "number-letter" divisions typically required an overall tally to determine the total number of test questions.

The favorite test was a one-page document. Rarely was a teacher-prepared answer sheet also required. Most tests were neat in appearance. Some were handwritten; others were typed. However, poor reproduction methods and overcrowding tended to make many tests hard to read. Between 15 and 20 percent of all the tests rated exhibited a grammatical, spelling, punctuation, or numerical error. Virtually all teachers used language in test questions that was judged to be universal and nondiscriminatory. In the rare cases that reviewers flagged as suspect, close study revealed evidence of sexual stereotyping.

Teachers' command of item-writing principles was related to the complexity of the item being constructed. Teachers who included multiple-choice questions on their tests usually stated the central problem in the stem, although many such items had only a one or two-word stem. The major flaw was that teachers did not arrange options in an apparent order. Teachers tended not to use true-false questions, but when they did, they presented them as clear, simple sentences containing only one thought. Matching exercises were frequent at all grade levels. Generally, the basis for matching was explained and homogeneous, brief lists of terms were presented. The tests reviewed exhibited several variations on the traditional models. One favorite variation was to arrange a large number of terms horizontally across the top or bottom of the top of the test sheet and to instruct students to choose answers to long sets of questions or fill-in-the-blank statements.

The most frequently used type of test questions was the short-answer response item. Approximately one half of these items appeared in the fill-in-the-blank style, while the other half required other styles of short-answer responses. One major defect of the short-answer response items reviewed in our study was ambiguity in the question. Another major defect was that several different responses could often be defended as correct. Very few teachers used essay questions. Less than 2 percent of the questions in the total sample could be classified as essay questions. The few essay items observed were clearly constructed, but they did not specify how much time should be spent in responding. Typically, essay questions are grouped at the end of a test.

What Do Teachers Test?

We gained some perspectives about teachers' practices in developing questions for classroom tests when we classified test questions by categories representing the student behaviors to be measured. Using the six behavioral categories delineated by Bloom and others (1981), we found that test items designed to measure students' knowledge of terms typically require students to provide short answers or to match supplied terms with supplied definitions. Given the relatively short length of teacher-made tests for the primary grades, few such tests presented more than one type of item and more than one category of behavior. Although this tendency may have arisen from teachers' concern about students' ability to handle different kinds of directions, it also may limit students' experience and practice with a variety of response modes. In the primary grades, many tests use oral instructions. The limited variety of test questions may be related to the amount of time required for presentation of oral instructions. Overall, knowledge of terms was measured by 16 percent of all the items that we reviewed. At least one in five of the test questions that junior and senior high school teachers designed fell into this category. The proportion rose to one in four for science and English teachers in junior and senior high schools.

Knowledge of facts was measured by 37 percent of all teacher-developed test questions in our sample. Almost eight out of nine questions in social studies tests for the junior high school grades and slightly more than seven in ten (73 percent) of the questions in social studies tests for the elementary grades fell into this behavioral category. These proportions can be contrasted with the 71 percent frequency of such questions in senior high school English tests. The high incidence of teacher-made questions in this behavioral category reinforces the concern expressed by Hills (1981) that tests should not measure how much students can remember but that tests often do little else.

As we anticipated, the bulk of items in tests for the elementary level (39 percent) focused on knowledge of rules and principles. Across all grade levels, 26 percent of the test items reviewed fell into this category, making it the second most frequently tested behavioral area. Elementary language arts tests in particular appeared to concentrate on rules and principles. At the junior high school level, more than 30 percent of the items in English and science tests fell into this category.

In our sample, mathematics tests both at the elementary and senior high school levels contained the largest number of tests questions measuring skills in using processes and procedures, since more than four out of every ten questions addressed these skills. Given the emphasis on computational competence, this outcome was to be expected.

Nine percent of the total number of items that we reviewed tested students' ability to make translations. Tests developed for senior high school French classes used large numbers of test questions that required students to translate words, sentences, and paragraphs from one language into another. In a few instances, translation from English to French was required. However, the greatest number of translations had to be made from French to English. Senior high school mathematics tests contained the second largest number of test questions in this category.

Eighteen percent of the questions in elementary school mathematics tests and 5 percent of the questions in senior high school mathematics tests measured students' ability to make applications. In contrast, elementary-level language arts tests and secondary-level English tests contained no questions related to this behavioral area. Overall, only 3 percent of the questions that we reviewed sampled students' ability to make applications. Virtual absence of questions targeted at this behavioral area suggests that instructional priorities are placed elsewhere. Undoubtedly, students must have skill and practice in order to do well on questions in this area. Because teachers were not requested to submit their plans or tables of specification along with their tests, we know little about their intentions in regard either to application questions or to questions tapping the other behaviors. Clearly, knowledge of terms, knowledge of facts, and knowledge of rules and principles provide the bases for understanding. However, students should also be able to use factual knowledge to make translations and applications. Given the very few test questions in our sample for the applications category, we conclude that teacher-made tests do not require students to display higher-order abilities.

Summary and Conclusions

District teachers can deal with many of the technical requirements for their classroom tests, such as arrangement of test questions and format of test pages. However, the general tendency to omit test directions and to use illegible test copies indicates a need for improvement. While legibility problems may result from lack of proper working equipment and appropriate supplies, teachers should still be concerned. Production standards for teacher-made tests need to improve, given our finding that almost one in five of the tests that we reviewed contained errors in mechanics and technical conventions, such as punctuation and spelling. That almost all the teacher-designed test questions were nondiscriminatory reflects teachers' sensitivity to issues addressed by the district's desegregation plan. The tests in our review tended to omit the point values to be assigned to test questions. This suggests that teachers may not be visualizing their tests as a means for quantifying students' performance as a measure of students' learning. This trend appears to confirm reports in the literature (Lazar-Morrison, 1980; Rudman and others, 1980; Yeh, 1980) that teachers' knowledge of fundamental measurement concepts is limited.

Teachers write more questions of the short-answer type than of any other type. They prefer fill-in-the-blank styles for this type of question. This tendency may reflect teachers' emphases on brief responses from students. The typical flaws of short-answer questions are ambiguous questions and several plausible correct answers. The second most favorite question form is the matching item, in which we encountered several variations. One preferred practice displays large numbers of answer options across the top or bottom of the test page. Teachers use few true-false questions and few essay questions.

While this may indicate that teachers lack skill in developing such questions, it may also indicate that teachers wish to reduce test scoring time, at least in regard to essay questions. The relative disuse of true-false questions may reflect an effort to reduce the preparation time required for design of effective true-false statements in a particular subject area. The rarity of essay questions, however, may imply that some serious questions about instructional priorities need to be raised. If these priorities discourage students from learning how to write cohesive discussions because instruction is focused on less complex behaviors that only require rote answers and regurgitation of simple facts, instruction needs to be redirected. Although questions that develop students' ability to think are desirable, Ebel (1979, p. 87) cautions that complex tasks presented by test items can have "some undesirable features." The more complex behaviors sampled by essay questions reduce the number of responses per hour of testing time, reduce reliability, and tend to be inefficient in producing accurate measurement per hour of testing. However, the essay void appears to support Datta's (1982) contention that data from the National Assessment of Educational Progress indicate that, while American schools have been successful at teaching students to formulate quick, short interpretations, they need to stress writing in all curriculum areas; such writing needs to require explanation, interpretation, and critical thinking.

The essay void in teacher-made tests is also significant if we look at the levels of behaviors that teachers require students to display in responding to test questions. Our findings present a picture of priorities: Questions requiring knowledge of terms come first, followed by questions requiring knowledge of facts and command of rules and principles. Information about the performance of students on the tests that we reviewed was not available, but we can assume that students had some success with such questions. Certainly, teachers would seek to develop questions that gave students a fair chance to pass the test, since such tests are based on teachers' classroom instruction. As Bloom and others (1981, p. 39) note, "For students, the objectives that really matter are those implicitly embedded in the tests on which their grades are based." Given these characteristics of teacher-made tests, the typical expectation is that students should provide short and quick answers related to factual knowledge. Applications, translations, processes, and products account for only one in five of the teacher-made questions that we reviewed. Although short-answer and matching questions can tap these behaviors, essay, true-false, and multiple-choice questions offer more viable possibilities for assessing higher-level behaviors. Our findings do not allow us to reach definitive conclusions about why teachers wrote the test items or chose to measure the behaviors assessed.

The picture of strengths and weaknesses that emerges from our review of teacher-made tests in the Cleveland school district seems to indicate that training programs addressing item construction and tests as measurement of student learning are desirable. Wanous and Mehrens (1981) report generally positive reactions by teachers to their "data box." That program and its activi-

38

ties received the approval of teachers who faced practical, everyday teaching testing problems, because it provided teachers with hands-on experience in improving their competencies in educational measurement.

We can conclude that teacher-made tests reflect what is valued in local classrooms. To the extent that the tests in our sample are typical, they provide needed perspectives about the strengths and weaknesses of teachers' application of educational assessment. Our view through the windows of teacher-made tests shows that instructional priorities aim for the most part at knowledge behaviors. Looking across grade levels and subject areas, we see that very few tests require extended responses of students. The essay void is everywhere. Although there are scattered hopeful signs, it appears that classroom tests and the learning that they examine require students to remember knowledge, not to use it.

References

Bloom, B. S., Madaus, G. F., and Hastings, J. T. *Evaluation to Improve Learning.* New York: McGraw-Hill, 1981.

Chambers, B. A. "Development and Evaluation of a Teacher-Training Package Designed to Increase Science Teachers' Classroom Test Skills." Unpublished doctoral dissertation, University of Maryland, 1979.

Chambers, B. A., and Fleming, M. *Test Screen: A Review Instrument for Teacher-Made Tests.* Unpublished document, Cleveland Public Schools, 1982.

Datta, L. "If 'How to Improve Schools' Is the Question, Are Tests Part of the Answer?" In W. B. Schrader (Ed.), *Measurement, Guidance, and Program Improvement,* New Directions for Testing and Measurement, no. 13. San Francisco: Jossey-Bass, 1982.

Ebel, R. L. *Essentials of Educational Measurement.* Englewood Cliffs, N.J.: Prentice-Hall, 1979.

Gronlund, N. E. *Measurement and Evaluation in Teaching.* New York: Macmillan, 1976.

Hills, J. R. *Measurement and Evaluation in the Classroom.* Columbus, Ohio: Merrill, 1981.

Lazar-Morrison, C., Polin, L., Moy, R., and Burry, L. *A Review of the Literature on Test Use.* Los Angeles: Center for the Study of Evaluation, 1980. (ED 204 411)

Quinto, F., and McKenna, B. *Alternatives to Standardized Testing.* Washington, D.C.: National Education Association, 1977.

Rudman, H.C., Kelly, J. L., Wanous, D. S., Mehrens, W. A., Clark, C. M., and Porter, A. C. *Integrating Assessment with Instruction: A Review 1922–1980.* East Lansing, Mich.: Institute for Research on Teaching, 1980.

Wanous, D. S., and Mehrens, W. A. "Helping Teachers Use Information: The Data Box Approach." *Measurement in Education,* 1981, *12* (4), 1–10.

Yeh, J. P. *A Reanalysis of Test Use Data.* Los Angeles: Center for the Study of Evaluation, 1980. (ED 205 590)

Margaret Fleming is acting special assistant to the superintendent of Cleveland (Ohio) public schools and a former director of research and development and deputy superintendent in Cleveland.

Barbara Chambers is manager in the Division of Policy Planning and Analysis, Cleveland public schools, and author of the Classroom Test Skills Teacher Training Package, *being adapted for publication by the Educational Testing Service.*

Tests and test scores have long been used to the detriment of minority children. Schools must chart their own educational course and use tests to assess students' and schools' successes in attaining their goals.

Testing and the Minority Child

Leonard C. Beckum

Despite the prominent role that tests play in our lives, few people really understand what ability and achievement tests are supposed to do. What is more alarming is that even those few psychometricians who profess to understand the purpose of tests disagree about things ranging from how to determine the appropriate norming procedure to the role that tests should play in making decisions about academic standing. If such disagreement exists among the most knowledgeable makers and users of tests, then we cannot be surprised by the despair that exists among the general public about the meaning and proper use of tests. This despair is intense for minority children and their families, who have been victimized by the abuse of tests and by the misuse of test scores.

Needs Met by Testing Programs

The modern notion of intelligence developed more than 150 years ago, about the middle of the nineteenth century. The movement began with the hypothesis that intelligence was determined by the size of one's head. The larger the head, the larger the brain and the higher the intellect. These three factors accounted for the differences among groups of people in social, economic, and political status. Scientists measured heads, identified racial and ethnic origin, and correlated those factors with the social, economic, and political conditions of the day. Samuel G. Morton, the great nineteenth-century Philadelphia physician and skull collector, substantiated the belief when he reported that the skulls of Caucasians were larger than those of blacks and

W. E. Hathaway (Ed.). *Testing in the Schools.* New Directions for Testing and Measurement, no. 19. San Francisco: Jossey-Bass, September 1983.

other groups. Scientists were satisfied that Morton had both justified the importance of skull size and rationalized the existing socioeconomic hierarchy of the races.

By the twentieth century, craniometry had been replaced by mental testing. Buoyed by the development of eugenics and driven by a continuing need to justify differences between the races, scientists set out to prove not only that class and race were arrayed in hierarchies of intelligence but that these differences were innate, inheritable, biological, and therefore unchangeable. Robert Yerkes developed an IQ test that became widely used. It was effective in identifying and stratifying the population of Americans entering World War I. It was used to curb the immigration of southern and eastern European races into American and to justify the subjugated condition of blacks. Gould (1981) presents a provocative analysis and discussion of Yerkes's work, its problems and limitations. He demonstrates that scores on Yerkes's IQ test reflect only the test taker's level of acculturation to American culture. Spearman, Arthur Jensen, and others have conducted controversial research that continues to rely on unverifiable concepts of intelligence while it neglects to resolve critical issues.

It is obvious that tests have met the need to maintain a scientific justification for differential treatment of various groups of people in this country. However, this is not to deny that tests have beneficial uses. For example, tests can assist school staff to plan educational programs, counsel students, and improve curriculum. Many school administrators at all levels, national, state, and local, recognize that test results are important for setting policy and for evaluating the results of educational programs. It is also clear that, despite criticism arising from the use of tests, school staff would be more susceptible to criticism if tests were not used. The serious question that we face today is whether the ways in which school staffs use tests help or hurt the educating of minority students. Minority educators believe that the impact of test use and misuse has been severe for minority students. The discussion that follows presents some of the major questions and problems raised about tests and the low test performance of minority students.

Issues Underlying the Low Test Performance of Minority Students

Many minority educators locate the beginning of test abuse and use of testing to the disadvantage of minority students in the late 1950s. In 1958, four years after the landmark case *Brown* v. *Board of Education of Topeka*, funds were appropriated under the National Defense Education Act for the testing and counseling of students. Up to that time, most people progressed through school without the aid of standardized tests. Schools viewed massive testing programs as an educational frill, too costly for their value to educational programs. But, with the legislation supporting testing and counseling, schools had the money to initiate new testing programs.

The haste with which the new testing programs were implemented established a pattern that continues to be one of the biggest problems created by school testing programs: the failure to provide the special training needed by staff in order to select and administer the proper tests and to interpret the results correctly. Teachers also need to have some general background relating testing to instructional design.

Minority Concerns. The developments outlined in the preceding paragraphs took place as the first desegregated classes were formed after the school desegregation order. Minority educators were suspicious of the movement to increase testing at such a crucial time. Since 1958, a number of test-related issues have emerged, which amplify that suspicion and concern. As the test development industry became well established, its concern for profitability appeared to outweigh its concern for matching particular test designs with specific student populations. The reader may wonder why minority educators have long criticized testing programs for improper norming, adverse impact, and general bias, yet test developers seem unable to correct the problem. Is the cost of developing tests appropriate for use with minority students prohibitive? Minorities continually raise this and similar questions, and the test industry has no definitive response.

Researchers' Concerns. Hoffman (1962) and Black (1963) were among the first researchers to criticize tests used with minority students. Their work led to investigations by Congress, to lawsuits in San Francisco and Boston, and to court decisions—the *Skelly* v. *Wright* decision in the case of *Hobsen* v. *Hansen*, and *Diana et al.* v. *California State Board of Education* (Leary, 1970). It wasn't long until serious misuse of tests was pointed out. Williams (1971) decried the administration of tests to black students when blacks had been omitted from the sample selected for test standardization as a violation of the three basic psychometric assumptions: validity, reliability, and standardization. In recent years, there has been an attempt to correct the problem. New norming samples include minorities, although some minority educators have criticized these samples for not including an appropriate percentage of minorities.

Misuse of IQ Tests. Perhaps the most egregious misuse of testing has been in classifying students for special education placement. In *Larry P.* v. *Riles*, the plaintiffs alleged in 1971 that black school children in San Francisco had been wrongly placed in EMR classes because of low IQ scores. Eight years later, federal court judge Robert F. Peckham held that standardized intelligence tests, such as the Stanford Binet and the Wechsler battery, had not been validated for the purpose of placing black children in self-contained EMR classes; that the entire placement process, including reliance on IQ scores, had resulted in disproportionate enrollments of black children in EMR classes; and the the defendants' conduct, in connection with the history of IQ testing and special education education in California, revealed an unlawful segregative intent. Since 1979, there have been some modifications in the court order, but the decision continues to cause difficulties for schools.

The Peckham decision raises two disturbing questions. The first involves the plaintiff's allegation that school district staffs have been motivated to use the test placing students in EMR classes not because such classes could provide the best possible education for the students but because the district received categorical funds in proportion to the number of EMR students. Thus, the formula established by the federal government inadvertently encouraged school staff to see benefits in having large numbers of EMR students, and placement practices justified by test results and encouraged by funding opportunities resulted in many years of unwarranted stigmatization for minority children.

The second disturbing aspect raised by the Peckham decision lies in the absence of interest and understanding among the public. Despite eight years of litigation and publicity, parents, educators, and the general public seemed not to understand the issues in the controversy when it began, and they do not appear to understand it much better today. Although most school personnel are now using other data to augment test scores, most still believe that tests are better than teacher records, observations from nonacademic activities, or information about capabilities demonstrated in nonschool settings to assess performance capabilities and students' needs.

Competence Testing. Another dilemma for schools has been raised by the issue of competence testing. Initiated in the late seventies, the competence test movement was an attempt to set minimum standards that students must meet in order to graduate from high school. In the landmark case of *Debra P. v. Turlington*, 3,445 black students filed a lawsuit because they failed the Florida literacy test. The original lawsuit did not include the 1,342 white students who failed the test. The judge decided that the case should represent all twelfth-grade students, black and white, who failed the test. The arguments in the case centered on the denial of high school diplomas to black students who had been subject to segregated schooling; the denial of due process, because the testing program was implemented after most students' schooling had been completed; and the impact of test results, which was tantamount to resegregation, because black students were overrepresented in the group that failed the test. In July 1979, the court ruled in favor of plaintiffs, ordering diplomas to be awarded to all students who failed the literacy test who were otherwise eligible for graduation. The court noted that the high number of black students who failed the test was a result of past discrimination and ruled that the test score requirement could not be used until the 1982–83 school year and that the school system had not given the students adequate notice of testing requirements before the test was given. This judgment applied to both black and white students.

The issue of minority test performance surfaced again over teacher certification tests in mid January 1983. Preliminary data from the new teacher certification test administered in California indicated that testees performed poorly overall, with 62 percent passing the test. For minorities, only 29 percent appear to have earned a score high enough to pass the test ("Many Would-Be Teachers...," 1983; Salter and Cline, 1983). Preliminary data concerning the impact of a teacher certification test used in Florida for the past two years are equally disturbing. The number of minority teachers hired has dropped from 666 in the 1981–82 school year to 494 in the 1982–83 school year. That 26 percent decline is almost twice the decline in nonminority hirings (Stein, 1983). With state certification processes becoming such a significant obstacle for minorities, it is obvious that the number of minority teachers in the classroom will diminish within a short period of time. The long struggle to provide role models in schools for minority students during their critical period of development will have been lost. While no one is interested in placing unqualified teachers in the classroom, the educational process to which young minority students are exposed and the tests used for certifying minority teachers must be questioned seriously.

How Test Data Inform School Personnel

The preceding discussion makes clear that test results are important to the decisions that national, state, and local school administrators must make about education programs. It is also clear that, however tests have been misused in the past, there are many constructive uses for standardized testing. Tests aid school staff in making decisions about the effectiveness of the school's educational programs, in identifying individual academic problems, and in prescribing remediation for academic skill improvement. However, heavy reliance on tests for these purposes has resulted in changes in the education system that go far beyond the stated purposes of testing. Tests have become so influential that many school districts adopt curriculum programs dictated by the content sampled by a given test. Districts believe that they must respond to pressures from within and without to have students do well on standardized examinations. This belief tends to confuse school policy makers and administrative decision makers about the legitimate goals of education. Teaching to a test creates an unnatural dichotomy between the learning of test-taking skills and a prescribed curricular content on the one hand and social skills, exploration, individual interests, and creativity on the other.

Testing and Ability. As a result of pressure by courts, minority educators, and researchers concerned about the tremendous disparity in test results between racial groups, test makers have incorporated checks for cultural bias into their methodology for test design. However, were it not for the advocacy of concerned educators and established researchers, the test industry would have maintained its self-perpetuated myth of culturally unbiased objectivity. Recently, the testing industry was challenged by research which shows that so-called ability test scores can be improved dramatically by training in test-taking skills. Belief in the validity of ability testing has been based on the assumption that ability tests examine cognitive abilities that are independent both of factual knowledge and of guessing. If students can learn to succeed on ability and IQ tests, there are dramatic policy implications for the use of tests for placement as well as for the need for instructional practices that can remedy poor performance on such tests.

Perhaps one of the simplest ways in which school staff can begin to reduce the negative impact of tests is to use test data in conjunction with other information available in the school. The failure on the part of defendants in the case of *Larry P.* v. *Riles* to use teacher observations, students' past performance in school, and performance in class assignments to augment the information from tests when placing students in EMR classes significantly influenced the judge's decision.

The individual who does well on tests in today's test-oriented education arena is somewhat like an athletic hero. Performing well on tests increases the individual's personal worth, raises expectations among school staff, and provides new status at home and among friends. And, good performance on tests effectively sets one person apart from another, serving as the rites of passage for the good performer and as a sentence to failure for the poor performer. Such reliance on test performance tends to ignore meaningful developmental considerations, such as readiness, time needed for mastery of skills, and late blooming. Moreover, it tends to create a condition in the schools that deemphasizes the importance of the learning needs of poor and minority students. The stigmatizing effects of poor test performance, coupled with criticism of the misuse of testing, tend to justify the suspicions that minorities have about the use of tests for discriminatory purposes. Parents are seriously influenced by their children's test performance. When parents are informed that their children have performed poorly on a test, they seldom if ever question the test itself. More often than not, the child and the parents will feel deficient.

Flaugher (1974) discusses this phenomenon in the context of misunderstanding and confusion about the function of tests. He believes that tests have three functions: to establish criteria for the purpose of selection and guidance; to describe the results of educational treatments; and to measure personal worth. When tests are used for the last function, performance on a test is seen not as an assessment of an individual's potential to succeed in a given context or as an indication of the success or failure of the education system in preparing students academically but as an indicator of the functional ability of the entire group to which the individual belongs. The impact of tests used for this function is particularly damaging if the child's score is low and the child is from a minority group or from a poor background. Clearly, the possible negative consequences of misinformation about tests and their use require local school personnel to take more responsibility for communicating with students and parents about test results.

Using Test Information in Counseling. One potentially valuable use of test information is in the counseling process. If test data are used to augment other information about a student's performance in school, such as the student's stated educational goals, employment interests, and family interest, test data will be more valuable to those who provide guidance and counseling. One of the most frustrating aspects of working with underachieving students lies in their seeming ignorance of the requirements that they must meet in order to take their place in the world of work. I worked with a group of sixth-grade students who tested approximately three years below grade level in reading and math. Most students in this group mentioned career interests that, given their academic performance, represented extremely unrealistic aspirations. Test information could be used to help such students prepare for the kind of careers to which they aspire. Indeed, test information should be used as a diagnostic tool to help point out skill development needs to parents, teachers, and child. Schools can then gain the commitment of parents and students to an instructional plan designed to help each child to attain his or her goals. Too often, school staff convey the impression that test data are useful and beneficial only in awarding scholarships; in determining college placement, special education placement, and district or school ranking; and in justifying appeals for federal funds. Schools must make it clear to the general public that they use test data to help plan individual learning programs that meet the needs of particular students.

Reasonable Expectations for Testing

Regardless of what some would have us believe about tests, tests only measure what a person has learned. We now know how much a fetus in the womb is affected both by internal conditions, such as the mother's diet and general physical health, and by external conditions, such as the environment in which the mother lives. The behaviors that an individual exhibits are an expression of learning that has taken place within a context of specific social, biological, and cultural conditions. It appears reasonable, then, to assume that tests are measures of learning and that test scores must be interpreted in terms of environmental, biological, and cultural factors that condition test performance. As Jencks (1972), p. 26) states: "In practice... all tests measure both aptitude and achievement.... If two students have had the same opportunity to acquire verbal skills, and if one has picked them up while the other has not, the test does indeed measure 'aptitude.' But, if one child has been raised speaking Spanish and another English, the test measures the Spanish-speaking child's mastery of a foreign language. If the Spanish-speaking child does worse than the English-speaking child, this shows lower achievement in this area, but it need not imply less aptitude.... When everyone is equally well prepared, achievement tests become aptitude tests. When people are unequally prepared, aptitude tests become achievement tests."

If learning basically occurs in a biological, social, and cultural context, learning is culture-bound. Since test design, test administration, and testee preparation all reflect biological, cultural, and environmental interactions between different parts of the social structure, tests cannot be culture-free. The content of tests usually reflects characteristics thought of as useful to maintenance of the dominant culture. Learning necessary to survive in particular subcultures or social environments may or may not be an asset in the testing context. Because tests are a reflection of the kind of learning and achievement that society values, learning acquired in environments that honor those values will assist test performance most. It does not mean that the child from a poor or minority environment may be deficient or lacks the capacity or ability to master tasks of a white middle-class environment but that the onus of operating in a less familiar world always weighs on the minority child. It does mean that the teaching-learning environments may have to be different in order to maximize the learning that takes place. It also means that inferences drawn from assessment procedures may have to be mediated by recognition of environmental differences if results are to be useful either to the school or to the child.

Because public education is an institution in which children from diverse backgrounds, ethnic groups, and abilities can be prepared to succeed, as measured by their movement along the social and economic continuum, it has been called *the great equalizer*. We know that equalization has not occurred for poor and minority children. While their failures have complex causes, the inappropriate uses of testing and the influence of testing in general on school curriculum have helped to mystify and even to perpetuate these failures. To a large extent, this means that the schools are not accountable to poor and minority children.

Conclusion

This chapter began by pointing out the absence of consensus within the psychometric community about the extent to which intelligence and achievement tests have overcome the superstitious origins and xenophobic intent of cognitive measurement. Research conclusions and the design of enrichment and remedial programs have evolved out of information provided by tests. The resulting programs have been ineffective in improving the condition of minority students. Blame has haunted the students, their parents, and public education as well. The stigmatization has contributed to the continued poor performance of these students.

We have arrived at a critical point in the history of education. Economic production is down, new technology is calling our concept of basic skills into question, and obsolescence is a daily occurrence in the workplace. Schools are challenged as never before to meet the emerging educational needs of a changing, less monocultural society. If tests are to be useful to schools as they attempt to meet this challenge, schools must begin by assuring that the important functions of academic diagnosis and placement, educational accountability, and communication about the meaning of test results are conducted equitably for all pupils.

References

Black, H. *They Shall Not Pass.* New York: Morrow, 1963.

Flaugher, R. L. "Some Points of Confusion in Discussing the Testing of Black Students." In L. P. Miller (Ed.), *The Testing of Black Students: A Symposium.* Englewood Cliffs, N.J.: Prentice-Hall, 1974.

Gould, S. J. *The Mismeasure of Man.* New York: Norton, 1981.

Hoffman, B. *The Tyranny of Testing.* New York: Crowell and Collier, 1962.

Jencks, C., and others. *Inequality: A Reassessment of the Effects of Family and Schooling in America.* New York: Basic Books, 1972.

Leary, M. E. "Children Who Are Tested in an Alien Language: Mentally Retarded?" *The New Republic,* 1970, *162* (22), 17–18.

"Many Would-Be Teachers Flunk New State Test." *San Francisco Chronicle,* January 14, 1983, p. 1.

Salter, S., and Cline, A. "Teacher Exam Put to the Test Because of 30 Percent Failure Rate." *San Francisco Examiner,* Sunday, January 16, 1983, p. 1.

Stein, G. "Does Florida Teaching Test Shut-Out Black Candidates?" *Miami Herald,* January 25, 1983, p. 1.

Williams, R. L. "Abuses and Misuses in Testing Black Children." *The Counseling Psychologist,* 1971, *8* (2), 62–73.

Leonard C. Beckum is executive project director for equity programs at Far West Laboratory for Educational Research and Development in San Francisco, California. His work on test problems includes design and development of tests for selection of police offficers in the city and county of San Francisco, review of school placement instruments in newly desegregated schools, and review of teacher and student assessment instruments for Educational Testing Service.

Conflicting claims by measurement theorists have caused confusion among educators, who want to apply the best available technology to their practical measurement problems.

Introduction to Latent Trait Analysis and Item Response Theory

Joseph P. Ryan

Significant improvements have occurred in educational measurement during the past decade. These improvements have come in many forms, and they have been influenced by a variety of educational, political, and financial forces. One of the most important improvements has been the development of procedures known as latent trait analysis and item response theory. These procedures provide educators with measuring instruments that are far more sensitive and accurate than the devices available in the past.

The one major obstacle to application of these techniques is the absence of a clear and simple explanation of what these procedures can do and of how they work when applied to practical measurement problems. This chapter provides an explanation of latent trait analysis and item response theory that will help educators to understand the philosophical rationale on which the procedures are based, to develop a conceptual understanding of how the procedures work, and to appreciate the difference between them. The chapter begins by examining the central concept of unidimensionality. Next, it discusses the difference between observed item responses and latent traits. Latent trait analysis is a procedure designed to measure unobserved or latent traits that can explain observed test performance. In contrast, item response theory focuses on actual

W. E. Hathaway (Ed.). *Testing in the Schools.* New Directions for Testing and Measurement, no. 19. San Francisco: Jossey-Bass, September 1983.

50

observed test performance. The chapter concludes that the procedures have different philosophical bases, that they provide different information when applied to test data, and that each can help educators to solve a different type of measurement problem.

Unidimensionality

The process of measuring psychological attributes requires us to assume that individual human attributes can be isolated and measured one at a time as if no other characteristic affected the attribute or trait in question. We must also assume that measuring instruments can be constructed that are sensitive to a single human attribute without being influenced by any other human characteristic. Together, these operational assumptions are often described as the assumption of unidimensionality.

The assumption of unidimensionality is not unique to psychological measurement, for it is also operationalized when such traits as height and weight are measured. When a physcial education teacher weighs students in a class, for example, the teacher assumes that the only attribute affecting measurement is the children's weight. The assumption of unidimensionality allows the teacher to order the students on a meaningful scale, such as pounds or kilograms, and to make decisions about an appropriate exercise or dietary program. Everyone realizes, of course, that children vary on many other characteristics, but when we measure weight we try to eliminate the effects of these other characteristics.

Unidimensionality is an ideal that is not always realized. For example, not all instruments can be used to measure all children. Furthermore, even when there are appropriate instruments, it is not always possible to measure all children, because the behavior of some children during the measurement process distorts the unidimensionality required to measure them appropriately. Recognizing this limitation of psychological measurement is not to admit inadequacy, since the same limitation is recognized by researchers in the natural sciences.

Experts in the field of psychological measurement have provided various definitions of unidimensionality. Here is one (Lord and Novick, 1968, p. 538): "an individual's performance depends on a single underlying trait if, given his value on that trait, nothing further can be learned from him that will contribute to the explanation of his performance. The proposition is that the trait is the only important factor and, once a person's value on the trait is determined, the behavior is random, in the sense of statistical independence." This interpretation of unidimensionality has two critical implications. Let us say that we know a person's reading ability. The first implication is that nothing else about the person will significantly improve our prediction of that person's performance on a reading test. The second implication is that the person's actual performance on any given reading test will not provide any additional information about the person's reading ability.

Observed Item Responses and Latent Traits

It is critical to differentiate between students' test performance as observed in their item responses and their underlying ability or relevant latent trait. This distinction is so critical that it will be illustrated here with a detailed example from a physical measurement situation.

Consider the test scores of five students on two tests of ten items. The test scores are shown in Table 1. On test A, Tom and Dale have higher scores than Bill, who scores higher than Walter. Loren, who has the lowest score, appears to have the least ability. The results on test B are not totally consistent with the results on test A. Tom and Dale both have higher scores than Bill, and Bill has a lower score than Walter, but Loren again has the lowest score.

In general, students make higher scores on test A than they do on test B. Test A must therefore be easier than test B. The difference between scores on the two tests is listed in Table 1. The average difference between test A and test B scores is three points. On the average, students' scores on test B are three points lower than their scores on test A. Thus, the scores that students can be expected to make on test B can be calculuated from the scores that they earned on test A: A student's expected score on test B equals the student's score on test A minus three.

The expected scores on test B calculated using this procedure are displayed in Table 1. Differences between the observed scores on test B and the expected scores on test B are shown in the last column. The sum of the differences is zero; hence, the average error in predicting scores on test B from the relationship between tests A and B is also zero for the five students. However, if we examine the differences between observed and expected scores on test B ignoring the plus and minus signs, a different result is obtained. The sum of the absolute values of the differences is $(2 + 2 + 2 + 3 + 1) = 10$. The average difference between observed and expected scores is ten divided by five, or two points. On the individual level, the procedure results in an error of two points; on a ten-point scale, this represents an error rate of 20 percent.

This detailed example reveals certain ambiguities that occur when we attempt to measure students by examining their test performance through

Table 1. Students' Scores on Tests A and B

Student	Test A	B	Score Difference (A − B)	Test B Expected Scores	Test B Observed Scores Minus Expected Score
Tom	10	9	1	7	2
Dale	8	3	5	5	− 2
Bill	7	2	5	4	− 2
Walter	6	6	0	3	3
Loren	4	0	4	1	− 1

observed item responses. These anomalies arise because in most testing situations students' observed scores reflect their unobserved or latent abilities only imperfectly. This does not mean that we cannot use test scores to measure students but that we must focus on something besides their actual item responses.

The confusion created by contradictions in observed test scores can be understood by examining the underlying and unobservable attribute of the students that we hope the test scores will reflect. Both tests in the preceding example are designed to measure students' strength in terms of their power to lift weights. The ten items on each test are ten different weights that each student is asked to lift. A successful lift represents a "correct answer" to the item, while an unsuccessful lift represents an "incorrect answer." The underlying and unobservable attribute of the students that explains the observed scores is their physical strength. Unobservable or underlying attributes are referred to as latent traits. A latent trait can never be observed directly; it can only be inferred from observable behaviors, such as actual item responses.

The relationship between students' performance on tests A and B and the latent trait that explains their performance is shown in Figure 1. Physical strength, the unobserved latent trait, is represented by the horizontal line at the bottom of Figure 1. The points on the scale are ordered from low to high, left to right, respectively. Lines representing observed performance on tests A and B are shown above the latent trait in horizontal positions that represent the respective range on the underlying variable that each test reflects.

Observed scores on tests A and B can now be interpreted more meaningfully, since we have now related them to the latent trait. Obviously, test A is easier than test B, since it spans a lower range on the latent trait. Loren makes a score of four on test A. This performance indicates that Loren has the ability to lift 90 pounds. Loren's score of zero on test B has no substantive meaning in the absence of additional information. A score of zero on test B indicates that a student's strength falls somewhere below the ability to lift 110 pounds, the lightest weight (easiest item) on the test. Independent of additional information, however, there is no way to meaningfully locate a person with a score of zero on the latent trait, since the person could fall anywhere below the lowest position reflected by test B. At the other end of the continuum, it is also impossible to locate the position of any person who makes a perfect score on a test. Tom has a score of ten on test A. This means that Tom can lift at least 150 pounds. In the absence of additional information, however, there is no way to measure Tom on the latent trait. From the results of test B, we know that Tom has the ability to lift 190 pounds, but this ability estimate cannot be made from examining the results of test A.

The performance of Loren and the performance of Tom illustrate a critically important measurement axiom: It is not possible to measure the latent ability of students who make perfect scores or zero scores on a given test. Certain statistical procedures can be used to extrapolate these scores onto the latent trait, but the results of these statistical manipulations are artifacts of the procedures, and interpretation cannot credit them with substantive meaning.

Figure 1. Relationship Between Observed Performance on Tests A and B and the Latent Trait Strength

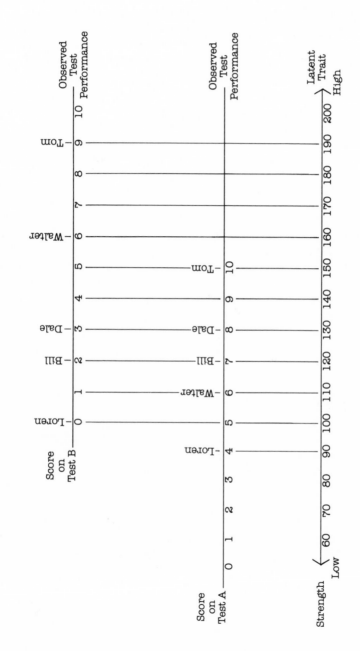

Walter's performance on the two tests provides inconsistent estimates of his latent ability. Does Walter have the ability to lift 110 pounds, or does he have the ability to lift 160 pounds? The inconsistency with which Walter's test scores estimate his latent ability is direct evidence that the operational assumption of unidimensionality has been violated. Violations of unidimensionality are due to the person, to the test or items on the test, or to the testing situation. For example, if Walter did not have a full night's sleep preceding test A, his performance on the test may not have reflected his true ability. Or the weights may not have been correctly calibrated when Walter took one or both tests. In such a situation, the inconsistent measurement of ability is due to a defect in the measuring instrument. Finally, Walter may have felt rushed when he took test A; hence, his strength may have been confounded by speededness. In any case, the explanation of Walter's inconsistent performance cannot be derived from his test scores alone; it can only be determined from other sources of information.

The scores of Bill and Dale on the two tests consistently estimate their latent abilities. Both test scores indicate that Bill has the ability to lift 120 pounds and that Dale can lift 130 pounds. Clearly, these latent ability estimates are independent of the test used to infer them. The scores of these students on test A differ from their scores on test B by five points. Figure 1 shows that the range of abilities spanned by the two tests also differs by five points at all points on the latent ability continuum covered by the overlapping tests. Thus, test A is five points easier than test B, not three points easier, as calculations based on the complete set of observed scores indicate.

In the preceding example, the students' test performance based on observed item responses represents the type of data examined in item response theory. Item response theory attempts to provide a statistically accurate description of such data. The mapping of observed performance onto the unobserved latent trait as well as the interpretation of individual students' observed performance in terms of the unobserved trait represent the types of activities that characterize latent trait analysis.

A certain number of important conclusions can be drawn from this example. First, strict substantive unidimensionality is required for measurement of the sort found in the natural sciences. Second, not all situations in which students' performance is observed meet the requirement of substantive unidimensionality. The situations in which students' performance is observed must be carefully controlled for measurement to be possible. In attempting to measure students' strength, for example, it would be advisable to have each student attempt each item in succession in order to minimize extraneous influence of endurance. Third, the performance data that have been collected must be examined carefully to determine whether the operational assumption of substantive unidimensionality can be accepted. Of course, this means that the operational assumption of unidimensionality is not an assumption at all; it is a hypothesis, the validity of which can be judged. Fourth, students with perfect scores or zero scores on a given test cannot be directly measured on a substantively unidimensional latent trait. Fifth, students with observed test scores that give inconsistent information relative to the latent trait, such as Walter, cannot be measured in a substantive sense. The performance of such students can be examined in order to explain such inconsistencies, but the performance data of these students cannot lead to measurements on a substantively unidimensional latent trait. It is informative to refer to such students as nonmeasured examinees. Sixth, latent trait abilities can be estimated independent of the specific tests administered, as in the cases of Bill and Dale. Seventh, certain procedures can be used to extract statistical information about students even if the hypothesis of substantive unidimensionality must be rejected. These procedures can be applied to students with perfect scores or zero scores and even to students whose test performance is inconsistent relative to the substantive latent trait. Application of these procedures can result in useful ordering of students on a statistically defined unidimensional scale of value in norm-referenced scaling. Such procedures can be used to make predictions from one statistically unidimensional scale to another. Application of these procedures, however, violates the hypothesis of strict substantive unidimensionality. Consequently, the results of such procedures limit the ability of educators to relate observed test performance directly to substantively unidimensional latent traits.

Latent Trait Measurement

The first step in the measurement process is conceptualization of the variable to be measured. Instructionally related variables are of particular interest to educators. These variables can be affected by instruction to increase a student's position on the latent trait. Such variables are of major interest to educators because the careful measurement of instructionally related variables is essential for accurate student diagnosis and placement, for curriculum development and reform, in the setting of educational goals and standards, and for instructional evaluation. Many other types of variables can be measured and studied, but those that relate to school learning are of primary concern.

A Geometric Representation. Let us assume that a group of educators is interested in measuring students' ability with respect to sixth-grade mathematics skill, third-grade language arts ability, or any other student trait toward which instruction is directed. Under the hypothesis of substantive unidimensionality, the instructional variable can be represented as a latent trait on which both the students and the items or tasks on a test can be ordered. This hypothetical situation is shown in Figure 2, where a simple horizontal line represents the latent trait. The amount of ability that a student possesses is reflected by the student's position on the latent trait. Students' abilities are marked above the line, with b_1 representing the ability of the first student, b_2 the ability

Figure 2. Hypothetical Latent Trait

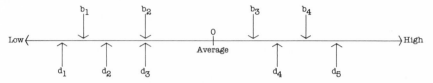

of the second student, and so on. The ability of the jth student or of any student in general is b_j. Item difficulties are marked below the line with d_1 representing the difficulty of the first item, d_2 the difficulty of the second item, and so on. The difficulty of the ith item or of any item in general is d_i.

The latent trait is drawn so that low values are on the left. Students with low ability and items low in difficulty values—that is, easy items—are located in this region. High values are on the right side of the latent trait; high-ability students and items with large difficulty values are found there. The latent trait scale is arranged so that the average value of the trait is defined as zero. This choice of origin is arbitrary, but it is widely used. With this choice of origin, students and items with below-average latent trait values are in the negative range, while above-average students and items are in the positive range.

The hypothesis of substantive unidimensionality generates three testable hypotheses: First only the ability of the students and no other student characteristic affects their position on the latent trait. Second, only the difficulty of the items and no other characteristic affects their position on the latent trait. Third, the trait on which the students are ordered according to ability is the same as the trait on which the items are ordered according to difficulty. Under these hypothetical conditions, it is informative and useful to discuss the probability that a student of some given ability will correctly answer an item of some particular difficulty. For instance, when a student with ability b_2 answers an item with difficulty d_2, the most probable outcome is a correct answer, since the ability of the student exceeds the difficulty of the item. When a student with ability b_2 answers an item with difficulty d_4, the most probable outcome is an incorrect answer, since the difficulty of the item exceeds the ability of the student. Finally, when a student with ability b_2 answers an item with difficulty d_3, the most probable outcome is unclear, because $b_2 = d_3$. In such cases, the student will sometimes answer the item correctly; at other times, the student's answer will be incorrect. The most reasonable probability to assign in such cases is .5.

These examples focus attention on the difference between a student's ability and an item's difficulty: $(b_j - d_i)$. The following three statements about the probability of a correct response for various values of $(b_j - d_i)$ are self-evident if the hypothesis of substantive unidimensionality is correct: If $b_j < d_i$, $P < .5$; if $b_j = d_i$, $P = .5$; and if $b_j > d_i$, $P = .5$.

A Mathematical Representation. Probabilities range from zero to one, whereas $(b_j - d_i)$ can range from large negative values to large positive values. Large negative values occur when very low-ability students answer very difficult items; large positive values occur when very high-ability students answer very easy items. Thus, $(b_j - d_i)$ cannot be interpreted directly in terms of the probability of a correct response. What is needed is a mathematical function of $(b_j - d_i)$ that allows it to be interpreted directly as a probability. Guided by the scientific principle of parsimony, we select the simplest function that meets this need. This function is called the simple logistic function and it has the form

(1)
$$F(b - d) = \frac{A^{(b-d)}}{1 + A^{(b-d)}}$$

In the simple logistic, $(b_j - d_i)$ is the exponent or power to which the base A is raised. The value of the base A is completely arbitrary. No matter what value is used as base A, the function always ranges between zero and one. In practice, the most commonly used value is the base of the natural log system, 2.7183.

We will refer to a student's response to a test item as X. The variable X can have one of two values: When the student gives a correct answer it is one; when the student gives an incorrect answer, it is zero. The use of the symbols b and d in equation 1 implies that values for ability and difficulty are known. To represent the more general situation, b must be replaced with β, and d must be replaced with δ. This notation indicates that ability and difficulty can never be observed directly but that they are estimated values or latent trait parameters.

Using this notation, the general model for the interaction in which students respond to dichotomously scored items is

(2)
$$P(X = 1 \mid \beta, \delta) = \frac{ex(\beta - \delta)}{1 + e^{(\beta - \delta)}}$$

To show how this model works, let us assume that $b = 2$ and that $d = 1$. For $X = 1$,

$$P(X = 1 \mid b = 2, d = 1) = \frac{e^{1(2-1)}}{1 + e^{1(2-1)}} = \frac{2.718}{1 + 2.718} = .74$$

and for $X = 0$,

$$P(X = 0 \mid b = 2, d = 1) = \frac{e^{0(2-1)}}{1 + e^{1(2-1)}} = \frac{1}{1 + 2.718} = .26$$

Two different names are commonly used for the model represented in equation 2: the one-parameter model and the Rasch model. It is called the one-parameter model because its mathematical form models one parameter of the item, namely, item difficulty. (The two- and three-parameter models will be described in a later section.) It is also called the Rasch model to acknowledge the pioneering work of the Danish statistician and psychometrician Georg Rasch. Rasch (1960) provided the first full exposition of the rationale and workings of the model. Rasch actually described a number of models. The Rasch model depicted in equation 2 is specifically applicable to the situation in which students' responses are classified into two categories, zero and one. Hence, the model depicted in equation 2 is the dichotomous Rasch model.

How the Model Works. Figure 3 and Table 2 show how the model works. The ability of thirteen students and three items on the latent trait are depicted. The abilities range from -3 to $+3$ in increments of .5, and the item difficulties are $d_1 = -2$, $d_2 = 0$, and $d_3 = +2$. The expected responses of students with the thirteen abilities to the three items are stated as probabilities in Table 2.

One very important feature of the model is that it is probabilistic, not deterministic. For example, the reader can locate the probability that a student with an ability of -1 will correctly answer the second item. According to the model, $P(X = 1 | b_5, d_2) = .269$. If any one such student responds to the item, the most likely outcome is an incorrect answer. If a hundred such students respond to the item, however, we can expect that approximately twenty-seven students will answer the item correctly. This result reflects the fact that the hypothesis of substantive unidimensionality is a simplification of complex reality and that it operates only within the limits of how people in general are likely to behave, not of how the individual student must behave in particular.

Using this simple procedure, we can calculate the expected number of correct answers for any group of students. The data can be examined, and the actual number of correct answers can be compared. The expected number of correct answers is based on the model, which in turn is simply a mathematical reflection of the hypothesis of substantive unidimensionality. If the observed and the expected number of correct responses agree within statistical limits, then the hypothesis of substantive unidimensionality is confirmed. If they do not, the hypothesis must be rejected, which means that some violation of the hypothesis has occurred. Thus, the model allows educators to test the hypothesis of substantive unidimensionality for any student or group of students responding to any item or group of items.

Figure 3. Latent Trait Representation for Information in Table 2

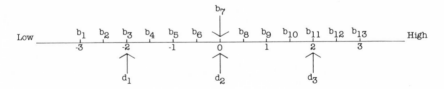

Table 2. Probabilities of Correct Answers for Students with Varying Abilities of Three Items

| Ability | Difficulty | | | | | |
| | (Item 1) Delta = − 2 | | (Item 2) Delta = 0 | | (Item 3) Delta = + 2 | |
Beta	(b − d)	Prob	(b − d)	Prob	(b − d)	Prob
b_1 − 3.0	− 1.0	.269	− 3.0	.047	− 5.0	.007
b_2 − 2.5	− 0.5	.378	− 2.5	.076	− 4.5	.011
b_3 − 2.0	0.0	.500	− 2.0	.119	− 4.0	.018
b_4 − 1.5	0.5	.623	− 1.5	.182	− 3.5	.029
b_5 − 1.0	1.0	.731	− 1.0	.269	− 3.0	.047
b_6 − 0.5	1.5	.818	− 0.5	.378	− 2.5	.076
b_7 0.0	2.0	.881	0.0	.500	− 2.0	.119
b_8 0.5	2.5	.924	0.5	.623	− 1.5	.182
b_9 1.0	3.0	.953	1.0	.731	− 1.0	.269
b_{10} 1.5	3.5	.971	1.5	.818	− 0.5	.378
b_{11} 2.0	4.0	.982	2.0	.881	0.0	.500
b_{12} 2.5	4.5	.989	2.5	.924	0.5	.623
b_{13} 3.0	5.0	.993	3.0	.953	1.0	.731

The Power of the Model. The power of the Rasch model lies in the fact that it provides us with a method for testing the hypothesis of substantive unidimensionality for every possible student–item interaction. The statistical procedure used to compare observed and expected frequencies is based on a chisquare analysis, which is part of elementary inferential statistics. Application of this procedure can fail to reject (confirm) the hypothesis of substantive unidimensionality. At the same time, the procedure can identify individual students and items for which the hypothesis does not hold. Ryan and others (1980) describe several examples in which the hypothesis of substantive unidimensionality proved untenable. In one classic example, on a sixth-grade language arts test a student with an ability of − .05 incorrectly answered six items with a difficulty considerably lower than the student's ability. One of these six was the easiest item on the test, which had a difficulty of − 2.114. According to the model, $P(X = 1 | b = − .05, d = − 2.114) = .89$. If the hypothesis of substantive unidimensionality had been correct in this case, it is highly likely that the student would have answered this and the other very easy items correctly. A brief conversation with the teacher indicated that the easiest items on the language arts test were read out loud to students because the items were designed to measure listening comprehension; the student in question was known to have a hearing impairment.

Estimating Values for Beta and Delta

We have yet to discuss how the values for student ability (β) and item difficulty (δ) are derived. An explication of the statistical procedures involved in estimating these parameters lies beyond the scope of this chapter. For purposes of this exposition, it will be sufficient to say that a difficulty estimate is derived for each item based on the proportion of students who answer the item correctly. However, if the substantive unidimensionality hypothesis holds, the final difficulty estimate for each item does not depend on the particular sample of students who take the test. This characteristic of difficulty estimates with the one-parameter model is often described by saying that the difficulties are freed from the specific sample used to derive them.

The process of estimating item difficulties is referred to as item calibration. After the item difficulties have been calibrated, they are used to estimate the latent abilities that correspond to each possible raw score on the test. Ability estimates are not derived for every student but for every interpretable raw score. The ability estimation procedure results in a simple conversion table that shows the one-to-one correspondence of each observed raw score obtained on a set of calibrated items to a unique latent trait ability estimate. If the substantive unidimensionality hypothesis applies, the ability estimate for a student is independent of the set or subset of calibrated items that the student attempts. This characteristic of ability estimates with the one-parameter model is often described by saying that the difficulties are freed from the specific set of items used to derive them. Students will generally make lower raw scores on tests composed of hard items, such as test B in our example, than on tests composed of easy items, such as test A, but the latent trait abilities estimated from two such tests will be equivalent within statistical limits if the substantive unidimensionality hypothesis is correct, as in the cases of Bill and Dale.

Item Characteristic Curves and Item Response Theory

The probabilities described in Figure 3 can be depicted visually with figures called item characteristic curves (ICCs). Item characteristic curves are drawn in a rectangular box; the horizontal axis represents the latent trait, and the vertical axis represents the probability of a correct response. Five ICCs are shown in Figure 4. The first three ICCs represent the first three from Figure 3. To see how ICCs work, locate the latent trait ability of -1.5 on the horizontal axis. Draw a vertical line from this point until the line intersects the ICC for item 1. From the point of intersection, draw a horizontal line to the probability axis on the left. The last line points to $P = .623$, the probability that a person with an ability of 1.5 will answer the first item correctly ($d_1 2$). The probability that students at any position on the latent trait will correctly answer any item can be determined in this fashion.

The Two-Parameter Model. Two additional ICCs are included in Figure 4. These represent the fourth and fifth items from Figure 3. The reader will note the difference between ICC_4 and ICC_2. ICC_4 is clearly steeper than ICC_2. When ability changes from $-.5$ to $+.5$, the probability that students will answer item 4 correctly increases from .10 to .90. The probability that stu-

61

Figure 4. Item Characteristic Curves

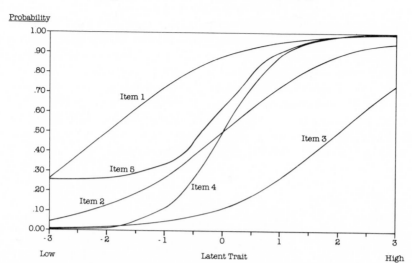

dents with an ability of − .5 will answer item 4 correctly is very low, meaning that the item is very difficult for students of this ability. For students with an ability of + .5, the probability that they will answer the item correctly is very high, meaning that the item is very easy for students of this ability. Thus, item 4 can discriminate between students in these two ability groups more sharply than item 2 can. Items with varying discrimination power are often observed in actual item response data. This observation has led many psychometricians to advocate use of a second item parameter in analyzing test data. This two-parameter model is written:

$$(3) \qquad P(X = 1 \mid \alpha, \beta, \ \delta) = \frac{e^{\beta(\beta - \delta)}}{1 + e^{\beta(\beta - \delta)}}$$

In this model, α represents the discrimination power of each item. All other items are defined as in the one-parameter model.

The use of the two parameter model presents two logical problems. First, the discrimination parameter is not used to model an underlying latent characteristic of test items. Rather, it is included because it provides a more detailed description of observed item responses. Second, inclusion of the discrimination parameter makes the interpretation of item difficulties ambiguous. For example, the probability that students with an ability of − .5 will answer item 2 correctly is greater than it is for item 4. Thus, item 2 must be easier than item 4 for such students. However, the probability that students with an ability of + .5 will answer item 4 correctly is greater than it is for item 2. Thus, item 4 must be easier than item 2 for such students. For items of widely varying discrimination powers, it is not possible to order the items by difficulty across the range of students' abilities because the relative ordering of the items is dependent or conditional on the ability of the subjects.

The Three-Parameter Model. ICC_5 represents another type of item that is sometimes observed in students' test data. The lower end of ICC_5 does not approach $P = 0$; instead, it flattens out and hovers at approximately $P = .25$. It is thought that ICCs of this nature reflect items that low-ability students answer correctly by guessing. If low-ability students randomly guess on a four-option multiple-choice item, approximately 25 percent of the students will guess correctly. Because item responses of this sort are observed in test data, many psychometricians advocate use of a third parameter in the model used to analyze test data. This three-parameter model can be written:

$$(4) \qquad P(x = 1 \mid C_g, \alpha, \beta, \ \delta) = C_g + (1 + C_g) \frac{e^{\beta(\beta-\delta)}}{1 + e^{\beta(\beta-\delta)}}$$

where C is the item's "guessability" and $(1 - C_g)$ is the probability of an incorrect guess. All other terms are defined as they were for the two-parameter model.

Because the three-parameter model includes a discrimination parameter, it contains the same problems inherent in the two-parameter model, but it has some additional problems of its own. First, the three-parameter model proposes that students can answer an item correctly by using one of two strategies: by applying their own ability or by guessing. It is difficult to see how a model that accommodates two strategies for answering an item correctly can be used to measure students on a single unidimensional latent trait. Second, it seems inappropriate to model guessing as a characteristic of test items, since guessing is more likely to be a characteristic of students. However, guessing is unlikely to be a characteristic either of items or of students, since few items evoke guessing from all students and since few students actually guess on all items.

Like the Rasch model, the two- and three-parameter models can be used to estimate students' expected responses. Expected scores based on these models can be compared with observed scores to determine the congruence between observed and expected performance. The congruence is usually greater for the two- and three-parameter models than it is for the one-parameter model, because these models include terms specifically designed to reflect observed item characteristics, such as discrimination and guessing. The problem with the two- and three-parameter models is that they generally match data more accurately, but they do not model the underlying substantive dynamics that explain the observed performance. For example, the three-parameter model will fit data reasonably well even if some students guess on some items. But the model cannot detect the student–item interactions in which guessing occurs, because the model contains a term that accounts for guessing. In this situation, educators cannot determine which items evoke guessing from which students. Ironically, the three-parameter model actually obscures guessing, because it is adapted to fit data and to minimize the difference between observed and expected responses. In contrast, individual student–item interactions in which guessing occurs can be detected by Rasch analysis, because such interactions represent a departure from the expectations of the one-parameter model.

Conclusion

The major thesis of this chapter is that latent trait analysis and item response theory are essentially different types of procedures. Latent trait analysis is concerned with measuring the underlying or latent characteristics of people. Item response theory is designed to describe and summarize observed performance statistically. Most psychometricians approach latent trait analysis and item response theory from a mathematical perspective, and that orientation can obscure the difference between the two. Consider the three-parameter model (equation 4) and assume that $C_g = 0$. In this case, the three-parameter model reduces algebraically to the two-parameter model. Furthermore, consider the two-parameter model (equation 3) and assume that $\alpha 1$. In this instance, the two-parameter model reduces algebraically to the one-parameter model. Examination of the three models in terms of their mathematical form leads to the conclusion that the one-parameter model is a special case of the two-parameter model, in which $\alpha = 1$, and that the two-parameter model is a special case of the three-parameter model, in which $C_g = 0$. The similarity of mathematical form obscures the fact that the particular form of the one-parameter model makes it uniquely able to test the hypothesis of substantive unidimensionality. The power to test that hypothesis is lost when the second and third item parameters are added.

From the perspective of applied mathematics, the difference between latent trait analysis and item response theory is not always easy to see. Innumerable studies have compared the results of test data analyzed with the one-parameter model to the results of analysis with the two- or three-parameter models. The results of these comparisons have been ambiguous; frequently, they are contradictory. The confusion is easy to explain if inconsistencies between observed responses and responses predicted from the one-parameter model are viewed as error in the statistical sense. If one makes the common assumption that such errors are random, we can expect that these errors will cancel each other out if there are large samples of students and if tests are long. What is revealed when the errors cancel each other out is the latent ability of the student and the difficulty of the items that explain the observed data. Thus, empirical comparisons of the one-parameter model with the other models yield similar results if the assumption of random error is tenable. If the assumption of random error does not hold, the results of such comparisons can be conflicting.

64

The necessary conclusion is that latent trait analysis and item response theory are based on different philosophical assumptions and that they have different purposes. When the two procedures are applied to the analysis of test data, they ask different questions. It is important to note that each answers its own question correctly. It remains for educators to determine which questions need to be answered for them to be able to solve their applied measurement problems.

References

Lord, F. M., and Novick, M. R. *Statistical Theories of Mental Test Scores.* Reading, Mass.: Addison-Wesley, 1968.

Rasch, G. *Probabilistic Models for Some Intelligence and Attainment Tests.* Copenhagen: Don Marks Pacdagogiski Institute, 1960.

Ryan, J. P., Garcia-Quintana, R., and Hamm, D. W. "Testing the Fit of Subjects to a Latent Trait Model." Paper presented at the annual meeting of the National Council on Measurement in Education, Boston, April 1980.

Joseph P. Ryan is an associate professor in educational research and psychology at the College of Education, University of South Carolina (Columbia). During the 1982–83 academic year, he served as a research associate in the Office of Research at the South Carolina State Department of Education, where he prepared this chapter.

Microcomputer technology can be used to improve both the efficiency and the validity of classroom testing practices while saving teachers substantial amounts of time.

Applications of Microcomputers to Classroom Testing

Ronald K. Hambleton
G. Ernest Anderson
Linda N. Murray

It is not uncommon to hear teachers complain about the difficulties that they face in preparing and scoring classroom tests. These complaints often center on their own limited test development skills, on the poor facilities for producing tests, and on the amount of time that it takes to do the work properly. But, help to classroom teachers who are concerned about efficient and valid classroom testing practices may be on the way in the form of item banks and microcomputers.

An item bank is a collection of test items that measure a domain of content; they are coded to make the task of retrieving them easier. Access to item banks can dramatically improve a teacher's capability for producing timely and valid classroom tests (Lippey, 1974; Howze, 1978; Jelden, 1982). To facilitate access to item banks, it is becoming common to store them in files in a computer. As for microcomputers, a popular operational definition is that they are inexpensive enough for a person to go to a store and buy one and small enough for the person to carry one home. Computers have been used in education for twenty years, but the microcomputers seem to be having an impact far in excess of earlier efforts. The low cost of microcomputers is a

W. E. Hathaway (Ed.). *Testing in the Schools.* New Directions for Testing and Measurement, no. 19. San Francisco: Jossey-Bass, September 1983.

primary reason. These machines are now showing up in schools in large numbers. Today, most secondary schools and a very large number of primary schools have at least one. As a sign of the times, one university expects all its students to have their own microcomputers by 1985. Combined with item banks, microcomputers can resolve many of the classroom testing problems that confront classroom teachers (Gleason, 1981). Fortunately, the amount of computer skills that teachers need to carry out their testing on computers is minimal; often, these skills can be learned quickly.

This chapter provides a brief introduction to microcomputer technology and discusses five uses of microcomputers in classroom testing: item storage, test assembly, test administration, test scoring, and test score reporting and analysis. It focuses on the testing applications of microcomputer technology. It does not discuss the necessary computer hardware and software in detail, and it does not discuss the many nontesting uses of microcomputers in schools at all.

Microcomputer Technology

It is common today to think of microcomputers as self-contained machines with the capability for processing binary data up to 64,000 bytes of storage. Such capacity will be ample for the instructional, testing, and record-keeping needs of most classroom teachers. Such peripheral equipment as disk drives, cathode ray tube monitors or screens, and printers are usually part of the standard auxiliary devices. Apple II, TRS–80, Commodore PET, Osborne, and Atari are five popular microcomputers.

At the beginning, a microcomputer was defined as a computer containing a very small chip of limited capability that could be housed in a small container and sold inexpensively. However, chips have developed in capability, while their cost has decreased substantially. Sixty-four thousand bytes of storage today take no more space and cost no more than 4,000 bytes of storage just one year ago. In addition, today's microcomputers run faster: Sixteen-bit microprocessor chips run much faster than their four-bit predecessors of not very long ago.

A look through any of the hundreds of new computer magazines will reveal that a large number of microcomputers exist for classroom use. How can schools decide which machine to purchase? Here are some questions that need to be asked:

First, can the machine be serviced readily and rapidly by a reputable dealer or repair service? Does the machine seem to need much in the way of repairs? What kind of track record does it have?

Second, does the machine have appropriate software and system programs that users like? Good data-based management, specific test item management and scoring software, or both will be needed. Also, a school will probably want a word processing package. Know What You Want and Try Before You Buy are good slogans today.

Third, how is the machine itself? It is easy to carry? Can it be locked up when it is not in use? Do you like the feel of the keyboard? How good are the graphic displays? Does it have color, or can color be added later inexpensively? Is the monitor screen display pleasing?

Fourth, is there a high probability that better software will be developed in the future? Do commercial software enterprises see a market for their products on the machine?

Fifth, does the machine allow for growth and expansion? Can a better monitor screen, a faster central processing unit chip, more memory, better external storage, and other devices be added? For testing applications, four options are desirable: a mark card or mark sheet reader, hard disk or other large storage for item banks, protocol communication with other machines, and a letter-quality printer.

Overall, at today's prices, a school will spend approximately $1,000 for a good microcomputer and another $1,000 to $3,000 for the kind of peripheral equipment mentioned earlier. But, while a school needs at least one microcomputer in each classroom, it needs only one of some of the more expensive peripheral equipment, such as mark card or mark sheet readers. It is not unreasonable to amortize the purchase price over a five-year period, since it is not unreasonable to expect the machines and attachments to last at least that long.

Item Storage

With the availability to teachers of banks of valid test items two of the major obstacles to valid classroom tests can be overcome: the time that it takes to construct quality tests and the inadequate training that most teachers receive in the area of item writing (Hambleton and others, 1982). Test items can be stored on disks and accessed by teachers or students through computer terminals or card readers on an as-needed basis. Some present computer systems allow test items to include graphics, motion, and sound. Computer-stored items have several advantages: Problems associated with test production can be reduced, and problems of item storage can be handled easily and conveniently, as can item revisions and new additions. Unfortunately, the existence of an item bank does not guarantee its usefulness. Items in a bank must be of high technical quality, and they must measure the desired learning outcomes validly if they are to serve a useful purpose. Inadequately stocked item banks will eventually result in invalid tests and misleading test results.

To be assured that an item bank contains valid items, two kinds of item reviews have been advocated: judgmental methods and empirical methods (Hambleton, 1982; Popham, 1981). Judgmental methods use teacher and content specialist ratings of items' technical quality and congruence with the objectives that they were written to measure. Empirical methods use inspection of examinees' responses to guide the process of item revision and review. The original test items can come from several sources: A number of item banks can be purchased from test publishers. Many school districts have compiled their own item banks; often, they are willing to share them with others. Many teachers have accumulated their own test items over the years, and test item–writing workshops for teachers can also result in useful items.

Three points need to be mentioned. First, test items can be stored on either hard or floppy disks. Floppy disks are easily transportable, but hard disks can hold substantially more test items than floppy disks. However, a single floppy disk can hold 300 test items. Second, comprehensive item codes are especially helpful in item selection. Items can be coded by format, answer key, level of difficulty, content, frequency of use, and most recent administration. Third, such item statistics as difficulty level and discriminating power can be helpful in designing tests to achieve specified purposes.

An alternative to storing items on disks is to store item forms, which can generate items at random (Millman, 1980; Millman and Outlaw, 1978). Storing item forms instead of the items themselves has several advantages. The most important is that the microcomputer can produce many more items than it can reasonably store (Millman and Outlaw, 1978). Very large pools of test items make it possible to produce a unique set of test items for each examinee. Under these conditions, it is not necessary for all students to take a test at the same time. Millman and Outlaw (1978) have reported successes with item forms in the areas of mathematics, science, and grammar.

A typical item form contains instructions on how to generate multiple test items. The instructions define the common and uncommon elements in the items. Each item has a similar item form. For instance, items can have a multiple-choice format, a similar stem, the same number of answer choices, and a common pool of distractors. An item form designed to generate multiple test items is shown in Figure 1. The complexity of the routines needed to develop multiple items depends on the content being assessed. It is considerably easier to write routines that generate items for low-level cognitive skills than it is to write routines that generate items for high-level skills. Clearly, the task could be made easier if measurement experts better explicated their content domains and if more creative programmers were employed. Millman (1980) shows how to develop and program an item routine for higher cognitive skills.

Test Assembly

A common complaint from teachers centers on the difficulty of assembling tests for classroom use. Directions and items must be written or edited, test material must be proofread, and a layout of the total test must be prepared for the purposes of copying. Microcomputers make test assembly easy. The test constructor can identify the appropriate test items and the desired item sequence from a terminal or from mark-sense sheets if a reader is available. Alternately, a routine can direct the microcomputer to select test items within

Figure 1. A Sample Item Form

Skill: The student can find the roots of quadratic equations of the form $ax^2 + bx + c = 0$.

Item Form:

    Solve for the roots of:

$$\{a\}X^2 + \{b\}X + \{c\} = 0$$

    where a, b, and c are randomly chosen integers between −25 and +25 subject to the condition that $b^2-4ac \geq 0$.

Answer Choices:

*(1) $\dfrac{-b + \sqrt{b^2-4ac}}{2a}$, $\dfrac{-b - \sqrt{b^2-4ac}}{2a}$

(2) $\dfrac{+b + \sqrt{b^2-4ac}}{2a}$, $\dfrac{+b - \sqrt{b^2-4ac}}{2a}$

(3) $\dfrac{-b + \sqrt{b^2-4ac}}{a}$, $\dfrac{-b - \sqrt{b^2-4ac}}{a}$

(4) $\dfrac{-b + \sqrt{b-4ac}}{2a}$, $\dfrac{-b - \sqrt{b-4ac}}{2a}$

(5) none of the above

---

a set of constraints provided by the test developer. The microcomputer can print one or multiple copies of the test. Before the test is printed, items can be further revised. To reduce clerical errors, the scoring key can be compiled from information referenced in the files for selected items. This procedure is more accurate than compiling a new scoring key and inputting it into the computer.

    A second approach to test assembly is possible when examinees are able to take their tests at the microcomputer. In that case, the examinee's performance during the test can dictate the items that she or he will confront later in the test. Adaptive testing is the name of this approach (Dewitt and Weiss, 1974; Lord, 1980; McKinley and Reckase, 1980; Weiss, 1982). More difficult items are administered to examinees who are doing well, examinees who are performing less well receive easier items. Since each examinee receives a unique set of test items, test security poses no problem.

70

Test Administration

When a microcomputer is available in the classroom for test administration, several options are open: First, the same items can be administered to every examinee. This option does not capitalize on the substantial capabilities of the microcomputer. Also, test security can become a problem.

Second, randomly equivalent forms of the same test can be administered to examinees. This option reduces the problem of test security, but it does not address individual differences in ability or specific informational needs that teachers may have for particular students.

Third, an adaptive testing strategy can be used to administer test items. This option is especially attractive when there is substantial variation in the ability of examinees, when tests are long, and when comparisons among examinees are of special interest. Since examinees receive different sets of items, comparisons cannot be made until the variations in test difficulty are corrected for. This can cause a problem. Models and principles from item response theory can be used to make the correction (Lord, 1980). To apply item response theory, item response model statistics must be available. This can require substantial field testing on reasonably large samples of examinees.

Fourth, test items can be administered to measure the objectives that a teacher wishes to have information about. This option has the advantage that a teacher can specify which objectives are to be assessed for each student.

Other options are also available, but the four just described are the most common.

Test Scoring

Classroom tests have long had ease of scoring as one of their claimed advantages. Teachers can check a one-position test response against a key to know whether the response to an item is right or wrong or that it has been omitted. A count of the number of right answers, sometimes corrected by a simple formula that penalizes for wrong guesses, produces a test score. However, hand scoring is time-consuming and somewhat error prone. This explains the interest in mechanical aids, which can score accurately, use formulas correctly, and even perform the item analyses that never seem to get done.

The first mechanical aid was, of course, the template that was placed over an answer sheet. Holes in the template corresponded to the correct answers. It was necessary only to count the marks that showed through the holes to obtain a count of the number right, after first ascertaining the numbers of multiple-marked items and omitted answers by hand. Electronics first came to the rescue in the form of the I.B.M. 805 test-scoring machine. Basically an analog device, it measured the amount of electrical current that passed through the marks that it was programmed to read. This machine had to be carefully calibrated at the start of each test-scoring session, and, if there were a large number of tests to score, it had to be recalibrated every few hours. Accuracy could be affected by the amount of graphite pencil that a student used in making the answer marks. But, the fact that tests had to be sent out to be scored meant that there was a delay in getting results. Most schools did not have one of these machines, and if they did, the typical teacher was not in a position to use it. Moreover, it was sufficiently hard to use that machine scoring of a small number of tests was discouraged.

Mark-sense punched card technology grew rapidly after World War II, and many schools installed I.B.M. Series 504 punched card machines for registration and student record purposes. At the same time, computers were being developed that could read cards punched in binary code and digest every bit, whether a particular combination of bits represented a legitimate character or not. The I.B.M. 1400 series of computers with column binary was the prime example of this technology. In the late 1950s and the early to mid 1960s, there was a sizable shift of classroom test recording to mark-sense cards, which could be prepunched with student identifying information and processed on a while-you-wait basis. The FAST system developed by Charles Wilkes in Richmond, California was the best-known and best-disseminated technology at this level. Sophisticated analysis could be an automatic by-product of scoring. However, it was still necessary to go somewhere outside the school to get tests scored, and publishers of the older answer sheets gramaced as royalties plummeted when the technology passed into the public domain.

The microcomputer has kept punched card and mark-sense card test technology alive and well. Inexpensive ($740) mark-sense card readers that attach to many microcomputers can take cards longer than the traditional I.B.M. card that record many more items on one form or that permit spacing that better matches the test itself. Even if cards have to be handfed (at the rate of twelve cards per minute), they make on-site and almost immediate scoring plus sophisticated analysis possible. Test publishers are beginning to provide software to keep student records of test results, to present class performance, and to suggest areas in which a student or a class needs to work.

The old test answer sheet has not been replaced by the punched card and mark-sense card technology for many tests and for many testing purposes. Large testing programs, many standardized tests, and even some local tests involve such sheets, which today can be processed in large batches on a variety of optical scanning equipment. The cantankerous old I.B.M. 805 test-scoring machine was replaced for large test scorers by such devices as SCRIBE (Educational Testing Service) and the Lindquist/Rulon machine in Iowa City that required precise paper characteristics (for example, the ability to expand in one direction only), humidity control (Iowa City clerks actually placed each answer sheet between fingers on a long conveyer belt to acclimate the sheet before it reached the scorer), and other restrictions that the average user could not manage. A new breed of optical scanner soon appeared. John Busby created the DIGITEK machine, out of which the OPSCAN Corporation grew. N.C.S. developed a reliable and inexpensive line of scanners, the smallest of which interfaces directly with a microcomputer; its price is in the neighborhood of $10,000. SCANTRONICS stand-alone scorers readily convert to data transcription devices today. These devices, which cost less than $5,000, can score a test and capture item responses, student data, or both for further analysis. The stand-alone scorers came into existence as the result of an effort to bring rapid and accurate objective test scoring closer to the schools in which education takes place. Today, with the general availability of the microcomputer and the decreasing costs of hardware and software, interfacing to a microcomputer is an idea whose time has come.

The advent of on-site microcomputers has eliminated some of the problems connected with use of the computer terminal: communication costs (telephones and lines), mainframe computer costs, and the vexing problems that can be created if the mainframe is not available when the teacher or student wants it. It is still too early to claim that every student has access to a microcomputer, but that time appears to be coming.

Test Score Reporting and Analysis

One common product of a test administration is a set of student test scores, sometimes a total test score, other times scores reflecting students' performance on a set of objectives. It is uncommon for teachers to carry out a complete statistical analysis of test scores or to evaluate test items. As a result, the teacher loses a considerable amount of valuable information. Figure 2 shows a typical student test score report, which describes the performance of an individual student in relation to the ten objectives measured by the test. Such reports can be given both the students and to their parents. Figure 3 provides one example of the many possible forms of teacher report. It displays the performance of each student in the class on each of the ten objectives in the test together with summary statistics on the students and the objectives. The microcomputer can also be programmed to use information about students' performance to provide instructional groupings. Figure 4 shows a report made for this purpose. Figures 2, 3, and 4 are reproduced with the permission of Educational Development Corporation. Another set of examples is offered by Crouse (1981). Space does not permit us to include other examples. Software is readily available for carrying out complete item analyses and test score analyses. The microcomputer makes it easy to combine item statistics for student scores on a particular test with item statistics in a master student file and to update the available statistical information regularly.

Summary

What might classroom testing be like in the future for teachers who have access to microcomputers? Here are some possibilities:

Figure 2. A Student Test Score Report

-Student Math Performance Report-

Name:	J. ARTHUR	School:	PEAK	Teacher:	JOHN SMITH
ID:	123456789	Class:	2G	Test Date:	APRIL 21, 1983
Level:	2				

No.	Math Objectives Description	Number of Test Items	Passing Score	Percent Score	Decision About Performance
2A1	Identify the number of objects in a group as odd or even.	8	75	100	Acceptable
2A2	Find the inequality symbol to relate two numbers.	4	75	75	May Need Work
2A3	Find the numeral for pictured hundreds, tens and ones to 999.	4	75	100	Acceptable
2B1	Read a clock to the nearest 5 minutes.	4	75	50	Need Work
2B3	Use a ruler to measure to the nearest inch.	4	75	50	Need Work
2B4	Use a ruler to measure to the nearest half inch.	4	75	25	Need Work
2E1	Add a two-digit and a one-digit number without regrouping.	4	75	75	May Need Work
2E2	Subtract a one-digit number from a two-digit number without regrouping.	8	75	100	Acceptable
2E5	Find the product of two one-digit numbers.	4	75	50	Need Work
2E6	Identify the sum of three one- or two-digit numbers.	4	75	50	Need Work

Summary of Test Performance

Statistic	Score	Objectives	Decision
Average Performance Level	68%	3	Acceptable
Number of Objectives Mastered	5	2	May Need Work
Number of Objectives Not Mastered	5	5	Need Work
Percent of Objectives Mastered	50%		

Figure 3. A Teacher Report of Student Test Performance

-Class Summary of Math Performance/Objective-

Teacher: J. SMITH
Level: 2
Students: 28

School: PEAK
Class: 2G

Test Date: APRIL 21, 1983

(Master = +   Non-Master = -)

Student ID Name	No.	Percent Score/Objective										Average Performance Level	Percent of Mastered Objectives
		2A1	2A2	2A3	2B1	2B3	2B4	2E1	2E2	2E5	2E6		
Arthur, J.	123456789	100+	75+	100+	50-	50-	25-	75+	100+	50-	50-	68	50
Burton, S.	023300000	75+	25-	25-	75+	100+	25-	75+	100+	75+	0-	57	60
Chang, O.	043300000	25-	0-	50-	100+	75+	75+	100+	25-	100+	100+	63	60
Diaz, R.	053300000	50-	75+	50-	75+	100+	100+	75+	75+	75+	50-	73	70
Frank, N.	063300000	75+	100+	75+	75+	50-	100+	75+	75+	0-	0-	65	70
Harvey, L.	073300000	0-	0-	75+	100+	75+	75+	0-	75+	75+	75+	55	70
Jackson, B.	083300000	75+	75		75+	75-	75+	75+	100+	75+	100+	79	70
Jones, M.	093300000	100+			75+	75+	50-	100+	0-	100+	100+	81	90
Kelley, E.	103300000	25-	75+	50-	75+	75+	0-	100+	0-	25-	50-	48	40
Rogers, W.	243300000	75+	100+	25-	75+	25-	50-	50-	25-	50-	50-	54	30
Sanchez, A.	253300000	100+	100+	100+	100+	75+	0-	75+	50-	100+	100+	82	80
Stone, T.	263300000	50-	100+	100+	100+	100+	100+	75+	75+	75+	0-	80	80
Washington, P.	273300000	75+	75+	100+	50-	50-	50-	50-	100+	50-	100+	69	50
Williams, P.	283300000	75+	25-	100+	100+	100+	100+	75+	100+	100+	100+	87	90
Number of Items		8	4	4	4	4	4	4	8	4	4	48	
Passing Percent Score		75	75	75	75	75	75	75	75	75	75	75	
Class Average		65	63	67	78	75	58	67	78	63	58	67	
Percent of Masters		40	43	47	55	54	41	50	55	40	38		45

Figure 4. A Teacher Report of Student Test Performance

-Math Groupings for Classroom Instruction-

Teacher: J. SMITH
Level: 2
Students: 28

School: PEAK
Class: 2G

Test Date: APRIL 21, 1983

Objective Number	Description	Class Performance Level	Students Needing Work			Students Who May Need Work		
			Number	Performance Level	Names	Number	Performance Level	Names
2A1	Identify the number of objects in a group as odd or even.	65	7	34	Chang, O. Diaz, R. Harvey, L. Stone, T. Kelly, E. Walter, B. Duck, D.	6	70	Burton, S. Frank, N. Jackson, B. Rogers, W. Washington, P. Williams, P.
2A2	Find the inequality symbol to relate two numbers.	63	7	49	Burton, S. Chang, O. Harvey, L. ...leton, C. Bird, B. Keon, D. Williams, P.	6	70	Arthur, J. Diaz, R. Jackson, B. Rogers, W. Washington, P. Williams, P.
2E6	Identify the sum of three one- or two-digit numbers.	58	9	41	Arthur, J. Burton, S. Diaz, R. Frank, N. Kelley, E. Mantle, M. Norman, N. Rogers, W. Stone, T.	1	75	Harvey, L.

First, the availability of valid item banks should serve to improve the quality of classroom testing. Computers can be programmed to select test items subject to constraints provided by the test developer, to generate items using appropriate item forms, and to print a set of selected test items from a bank. Second, because microcomputers make test construction much easier, testing can be more frequent, and it can be tailored to the skills of individual students and to their location in a curriculum. Numerous studies have reported that it is desirable to provide both teachers and students with more information about student progress. Third, microcomputers allow teachers to spend much less time writing items, assembling tests, and scoring answer sheets. Fourth, with almost no effort, teachers can obtain score distributions, item analyses, and reliability information for each test. Fifth, microcomputers make it easy to keep accurate records of student test performance over time. Sixth, tests can be quickly scored; this facilitates immediate feedback to students and teachers. Seventh, problems of test security are reduced substantially, because multiple forms of any test can easily be produced. Eighth, literally an infinite number of test variations are available for retesting students who failed an earlier test or for assessing students who were absent on the day of test administration. Ninth, adaptive testing is especially useful in placement testing, norm-referenced testing, and instructional testing within the context of hierarchies of learning objectives. It can reduce testing time substantially. Tenth, item files can be regularly revised and extended, and they need not be limited to objective formats. However, nonobjective formats, such as short-answer, sentence, completion, and essay, will continue to require noncomputer scoring. Eleventh, the microcomputer can pace students, allowing just so much time for a question. Twelfth, the microcomputer can control the items that a student responds to at a given time, preventing the student from returning to the item, for example, or making the student reconsider an item incorrectly responded to. Finally, the microcomputer can also control the item difficulty level: By skipping items that appear to be too easy for the student and by avoiding items that appear to give the student too low a success rate, the computer can zero in on the student's ability or achievement level.

Many of the ideas just presented are not new. What is new is the economic as well as the technical feasibility of large-scale implementation. We expect to see substantial improvements in the quality of classroom testing in the next few years as a result of microcomputers.

References

Crouse, D. B. "The Computerized Gradebook as a Component of a Computer-Managed Curriculum." *Educational Technology*, 1981, *21*, 16–20.

Dewitt, L. J., and Weiss, D. J. *A Computer Software System for Adaptive Ability Measurement.* Research Report 74–1. Minneapolis: Department of Psychology, University of Minnesota, 1974.

Gleason, G. T. "Microcomputers in Education: The State of the Art." *Educational Technology*, 1981, *21*, 7–18.

Hambleton, R. K. "Advances in Criterion-Referenced Testing Technology." In C. Reynolds and T. Gutkin (Eds.), *Handbook of School Psychology*. New York: Wiley, 1982.

Hambleton, R. K., Murray, L. N., and Anderson, J. *Evaluating Criterion-Referenced Test Items: Some Practical Techniques.* Technical Report 82–1. Vancouver: Educational Research Institute of British Columbia, 1982.

Howze, G. "An Interactive Software System for Computer-Assisted Testing." *AEDS Journal*, 1978, *11*, 31–37.

Jelden, D. L. "Computer-Generated Testing." *AEDS Monitor*, 1982, *20*, 32–35.

Lippey, G. (Ed.). *Computer-Assisted Test Construction.* Englewood Cliffs, N.J.: Educational Technology Publications, 1974.

Lord, F. M. *Applications of Item Response Theory to Practical Testing Problems.* Hillsdale, N.J.: Erlbaum, 1980.

McKinley, R. L., and Reckase, M. D. "Computer Applications to Ability Testing." *AEDS Journal*, 1980, *13*, 193–203.

Millman, J. "Computer-Based Item Generation." In R. Berk (Ed.), *Criterion-Referenced Measurement: The State of the Art.* Baltimore: Johns Hopkins University Press, 1980.

Millman, J., and Outlaw, W. S. "Testing by Computer." *AEDS Journal*, 1978, *11*, 57–72.

Popham, W. J. *Modern Educational Measurement.* Englewood Cliffs, N.J.: Prentice-Hall, 1981.

Schaefer, E., and Marschall, L. A. "Design and Use of a Computerized Test-Generating Program." *American Journal of Physics*, 1980, *48*, 518–522.

Weiss, D. J. "Improving Measurement Quality and Efficiency with Adaptive Testing." *Applied Psychological Measurement*, 1982, *6*, 473–492.

Ronald K. Hambleton is professor of education and psychology and chairperson of the Laboratory of Psychometric and Evaluative Research at the University of Massachusetts, Amherst.

G. Ernest Anderson is professor of education at the University of Massachusetts, Amherst.

Linda N. Murray is a research associate and graduate student at the University of Massachusetts, Amherst.

This chapter shows how one large urban school district makes
test scores meaningful to schools and understandable to the public.

A Case Study: Testing in the Albuquerque Public Schools

Carol Robinson

This chapter is a case study of testing in the Albuquerque public schools, currently the twenty-seventh largest school district in the nation. The district's department of instructional research, testing, and evaluation (IRTE) was formed in fall 1979. Prior to that time, the district employed several evaluation specialists (now called district program evaluators), each of whom reported to a different department or area office in the district. As the need for credible and consistent testing and assessment became greater and as test scores became increasingly important to the public, the formation of a centralized department became necessary.

The reorganization to create a centralized department required the reassignment of existing evaluation specialists not only to a new location but also to a new supervisor. As with any reorganization, there were growing pains. For example, it was quickly discovered that the professionals who served in the newly organized department had many strongly diverse viewpoints on all areas of assessment.

In the effort to create one centralized district unit, certain concerns became paramount. First, even though all schools were participating in state-mandated assessment, policies regarding standardized testing procedures and possible student exemptions were not consistently followed. Second, the district had three areas. Each area received test data compiled in a different

W. E. Hathaway (Ed.). *Testing in the Schools.* New Directions for Testing
and Measurement, no. 19. San Francisco: Jossey-Bass, September 1983.

format and the reports disseminated to individual schools were area reports, not district reports. Thus, it was not feasible to develop a district profile of test results. Third, curriculum center content area leaders acting in isolation were writing and mandating tests without benefit of statistical expertise or technical experience in test development. Fourth, the assistance that individual schools received in understanding and applying testing information was inconsistent in quantity, quality, and approach. Fifth, the Albuquerque community was essentially uninformed about and frequently suspicious of student achievement in the schools. Sixth, many teachers and administrators felt that testing was both too time-consuming and lacking in practical applications for improvement of the instructional program. These individuals strongly encouraged the district to move quickly to adopt a district testing program and to curtail the proliferation of content area tests by well-meaning curriculum coordinators. Seventh, upper administration had concerns about the amount of money being spent outside the state for scoring contracts negotiated by the state department of education. These individuals wished to move quickly to develop the in-house scoring potential that they felt existed within the district. Finally, researchers working on the master's thesis or the doctoral dissertation frequently administered tests that were unnecessary or objectionable to parents, teachers, counselors, or administrators. Once such projects were approved, infrequent or inadequate monitoring procedures contributed to the continuation of such projects.

At this writing, the IRTE department is beginning its fourth year of operation. A great deal has been accomplished, but much still remains to be done. The remainder of this case study will focus on three areas that reflect specific efforts and outcomes.

Department Procedures

The position of district coordinator of testing was created to improve the consistency of testing in-service, procedures, and reporting. In spring 1981, the district successfully scored the state-mandated Comprehensive Tests of Basic Skills (CTBS) for fifth-grade students. Scoring for eighth-grade students was added in spring 1982 and for third-grade students in spring 1983. Thus, all grade levels that have been required to test by state mandate will be scored in-house by spring 1983. All testing for Chapter 1 (previously Title I) elementary schools in now being scored in-house. New programs will be written to score new tests introduced in spring 1983. Testing required by state mandate for students in the state elementary bilingual program will be scored in-house in spring 1983.

Tapes are purchased from scoring agencies when scoring cannot be accomplished in-house, as in the case of the New Mexico High School Proficiency Examination, which is a customized secure test developed annually from an item bank by an out-of-state contractor. These computer tapes are analyzed, graphed, and reviewed with school and program administrators.

Computer tapes are secured for test results of the Preliminary Scholastic Aptitude Test, which is also used as the National Merit Scholarship qualifying test. This information is analyzed and reported to schools for use in improving their instructional programs for college-bound high school students.

District program evaluators are assigned to work with individual curriculum center content coordinators. The team approach ensures quality coordination and evaluation of program and assessment. An advisory committee made up of teachers and counselors representing all three areas of the district and all three instructional levels (elementary, middle school, and high school) has been formed to advise the director of instructional research, testing and evaluation and the district coordinator of testing about staff concerns and views on testing. District policies regarding testing have been reviewed and rewritten. New policies have been written where necessary, using input from the testing and evaluation advisory committee. Finally, the entire process for approval of proposed research in the Albuquerque Public Schools has been reviewed and revised. New procedures and guidelines have been adopted to guard against inappropriate testing of students as a result of external research.

District Evaluation Services

Since services to the district's 112 schools varied so widely in the past in both approach and degree and since as many as 20 percent of the principals in the district are transferred to new schools each year, the first task of the new IRTE department was to establish a data base that would assist the IRTE professional staff in looking at just how well they were communicating with each school on testing and other matters and to provide them with an overview, based on hard data, of the nature and number of contacts with each school and of the types of requests that were being made by principals, counselors, teachers, and other staff members. The latter goal has been met through a computerized system that summarized information on a form that records each school contact and its purpose.

Another key feature of the district's evaluation services plan involves the district program evaluators (DPEs). DPEs had worked with district schools for several years, but each DPE had his or her own ideas about testing and his or her own priorities regarding what schools needed. The district's new school evaluation services plan identified one DPE as the coordinator, and five others were named to work with specified schools. The coordinator of district testing and the DPEs assigned to the Chapter 1 schools also participated in this project. The percentage of time spent in school evaluation services ranges from 10 to 50 percent of each professional evaluator's work load.

Dissemination of Test Results and Applications of Testing

In the recent past, metropolitan school districts have recognized that the public image of schools depends largely on selective media portrayal.

Media coverage of Albuquerque's public schools has been much like the coverage in many large urban areas, where the media, especially the printed media, tend to take a sensational or controversial approach and rarely report the district's good news. For several years, a number of district administrators have worked with media personnel in an effort to broaden their scope to the positive aspects of Albuquerque's schools and the educational process. A public information office was formed, headed by a director of public information who communicated with reporters, writers, and various newspaper, radio, and television staff. These efforts have resulted in better working relationships with the various media. However, the problem of negative press created by inaccurate or incomplete reporting continues to cause concern.

Negative press was especially noticeable in the reporting of test scores. The IRTE department experimented with various reporting procedures and went to great lengths to educate reporters about the strengths and weaknesses of testing, the terminology that was necessary to understand test scores, and the meaning and uses of test data. IRTE staff hoped that reporters would gain an understanding that would then be reflected in more objective reporting and that would include information pertinent to a true understanding of testing. This did not happen. Despite all efforts by IRTE personnel, some reporters continued to dwell on the sensational, reporting that half the city's schools were below the national average when half the city's schools were above the national average. Or, when scoring problems were encountered with an outside scoring contractor, headlines would accuse the district of "hiding" or "delaying" information, which implied that scores had dropped or that they were very bad.

After several years of frustration in this regard, the IRTE department developed a plan of dissemination in conjunction with the district office of public information that was geared toward informing the public about testing. The plan was established not just to report test scores but to make the public more knowledgeable about testing as an instructional tool. The plan involved the production and distribution by the school system of testing reports formulated as daily newspaper inserts. The inserts are called "APS in Action." They are written and edited by IRTE and the public information office, working jointly. Ten thousand copies of "APS in Action" are distributed to local citizens as an insert in the Sunday morning issue of the metropolitan area newspaper. The insert format uses questions about testing that are of interest to the general public and it gives answers in nontechnical language. Brief editorial columns by the superintendent of schools are also included. In an effort to solicit the involvement and support of parents, information on how parents can help children prepare for major tests, such as those used for state assessment, is provided. Parents are encouraged to discuss helpful hints with students prior to testing. A calendar of major testing dates is provided, so that parents can be sure that children are in school, healthy, and that they receive a good night's sleep the night before. Other reports including more technical data are prepared and distributed to district employees and other interested readers.

Each academic year, the state assessment plan mandates testing of all students in three grades (formerly grades 5, 8, and 11; in 1983, testing will include grades, 3, 5, and 8) with a standardized norm-referenced test. The state assessment test for grades 5, 8, and 11 is included in the media distribution plan, along with a complete report of results on how well district students do on college entrance examinations.

Press conferences are planned to coincide with the release of the special testing issues of "APS in Action." Timing is crucial, as competition is keen in the media industry and as it is important for the press conference to be held as close to the release of the Sunday insert as possible. For these reasons, most press conferences are planned for Thursday or Friday. Articles by reporters are released Friday and Saturday, and the district's insert appears in the Sunday morning newspaper. At press conferences, test scores are reviewed, and the terminology, technical specifics, and applications to improvement of instruction are explained. Reporters who attend the press conferences receive an early release copy of "APS in Action" as well as a district test report and other pertinent information. The formal explanation of test scores at press conferences lasts thirty minutes, and an open question-and-answer session follows. A panel consisting of the superintendent of schools, the president of the board of education, the director of instructional research, testing, and evaluation, and the district coordinator of testing answers questions about testing, curriculum, and plans for curricular change; explains why test scores are high or low; and responds to technical inquiries and other matters of concern.

Reports of the press conference are typically seen on local evening television news broadcasts, heard on various radio news reports, and reported in the morning and evening newspapers. In addition, several reporters often request brief interviews with one or more panel members. These interviews are aired by radio and television stations, including the local Public Broadcasting System station, or they are quoted in newspaper articles.

Reports from our many parent and community advisory committees are encouraging. The information that we receive suggests that the Albuquerque community now has a much better understanding of the testing program as well as an ability to see it in broader perspective. Where once we dealt defensively with public outcry over uninterpretable means and medians, we now find ourselves answering questions about the changes in instruction that may have caused scores to increase or decline. In general, we feel that the Albuquerque community not only has a better understanding of the testing program and of the strengths and limitations of testing, but the community has a better attitude toward the schools in general. When the district began to release and discuss the results of the testing program openly, the community responded with an increased level of trust and, according to many, the district's overall credibility has improved.

The district's decision to develop its own documents to explain testing, rather than to depend on possibly biased reporting by the media, has paid off in many ways. For the 1983–84 school year, the district plans to continue this method of reporting and dissemination. Modifications to the plan will be made after a thorough review of specifics regarding the plan for this year. It is the general feeling of district administrators and board of education members as well as advisory board members that the public dissemination plan developed by the IRTE and public information departments of the Albuquerque public schools has great merit and that it has brought about increased and more positive understanding of educational measurement by the public. Developing a cooperative relationship between the public school district that desires complete and accurate use of a multiplicity of information and the media that desire to satisfy a public need to know leads to better understanding and to improved feeling and community consciousness about assessment in the public schools.

Carol Robinson is director of the Department of Instructional Research, Testing, and Evaluation in the Albuquerque public schools. Prior to her present position, she served as a teacher and counselor in grades K–12 and as an evaluation specialist.

This chapter describes how one of our nation's largest urban school systems works through the complexities of diverse testing programs, testing schedules, and students to produce timely results that help students, parents, teachers, administrators, and policy makers to make sound decisions about learning.

A Case Study: Testing in the Los Angeles Public Schools

Floraline Stevens
Marilyn Burns

Testing in the Los Angeles Unified School District is a study in complexity. The complexity comes in part from the numbers: The district has a half million students in 700 schools, and there are approximately 40,000 students at each grade level. It comes in part from having more than 100,000 students who are limited-English-proficient (LEP). It comes in part from having a year-round school program in one third of its schools to relieve overcrowding, whereas the testing schedule must serve both regular and year-round schools. And, it comes in part from the many layers of testing needed to meet federal, state, and local district requirements for information on student achievement. Nevertheless, testing in this large urban school district is successful, due to good planning and good communication by the district's testing unit and to the professionalism and commitment of certificated staff in the schools.

Multiple Testing Programs

Approximately 120,000 pupils in grades 3, 6, and 12 are tested for the California Assessment Program (CAP) in reading, math, spelling, and language. Since this is a matrix sampling assessment and there are several forms of the test, there are no individual pupil scores; instead, aggregated scores are

W. E. Hathaway (Ed.). *Testing in the Schools.* New Directions for Testing and Measurement, no. 19. San Francisco: Jossey-Bass, September 1983.

86

converted into average percent correct or scale scores. Another testing program for grades 5, 7, and 10 is the Physical Performance Test (PPT). PPT scores are reported to the district board of education and filed for future reference. To meet the requirement of Assembly Bill 65 (AB 65) for competence test requirements and local district information, the district developed a series of criterion-referenced tests. With district assistance, the Southwest Regional Laboratory developed the Survey of Essential Skills (SES), a series of tests in reading, math, and language skills for grades 1 through 6. Writing skills tests were developed for grades 3 and 6 only. To meet the state competence requirements SES student scores are reported for grade 5. In grades 7 and 10, the district developed tests in reading, math and writing (PAIR, ASC, and WRITE:Jr for junior high schools; SHARP, TOPICS, and WRITE: Sr for senior high schools) as part of the AB 65 requirement. A student must pass all three senior high school tests in order to receive a high school diploma. Students who do not pass the tests in grade 10 can be retested in grades 11 and 12 after taking remediation classes. Both the state and federal governments also require all students whose home language is other than English to be tested for oral English proficiency. Students new to the district are tested with the Basic Inventory of Natural Language (BINL) within thirty days of the start of the school year. Students who enter after the first thirty days must take the BINL within ten days of enrollment.

The federal government, through the state, requires achievement test information for students in compensatory education (Chapter 1) and bilingual programs. Survey of Essential Skills scores for English-proficient students in grades 1 through 6 are converted into equated norm-referenced percentile scores. Each version of the SES was equated with the Comprehensive Tests of Basic Skills, Form S (CTBS–S). At the secondary level, the CTBS–S is given to compensatory education students. Limited-English-proficient Spanish-speaking students who have not had six months of English reading are administered the CTBS–Español. Since no norm-referenced tests are available for the four other major language groups (Cantonese, Armenian, Korean, and Vietnamese), these LEP students are not tested. The compensatory education and bilingual education program tests scores are transmitted to the state on tape because of the large number of students involved in these testing programs. The district's norm-referenced testing program uses the CTBS–S to evaluate students in grades 3, 5, and 8 in reading and math. Students in grades 6 and 11 can be tested in reading and math at the school's option. Individual pupil data (raw score, percentile, and stanine) are provided as well as region and district results using median percentile to indicate achievement for each category.

Multiple Testing Schedules

Regular Schools. At the beginning of each school year, a testing schedule is planned for all schools on the regular schedule, in which ten school months of instruction are followed by a summer vacation. All except one of the mandated testing programs occur in the spring. The testing schedule must take into account the test time requirement, the time it takes teachers to code answer documents, and the time it takes to clean up and prepare the documents for scoring. Each year, the state specifies a time period for California Assessment Program tests, and the schedules for other tests must be fitted on either side of the CAP schedule.

Another consideration in scheduling is the handling and preparation of answer documents after they leave the school. Just as it prevents problems to have schools use only one type of test material in a given time span, the packaging, trucking, and scanning of different answer documents must be strictly separated as materials from schools flow through the scoring and report production processes. The materials from elementary, junior high, and senior high schools must all fit into the single processing flow. In the past three years, more than 800,000 answer documents have been processed yearly — most of them in the second half of the spring semester. The testing schedule for regular schools is designed so that each test and each grade level maintains its separate identity within the flow.

Year-Round Schools. During the past few years, some district schools have become overcrowded, and staff members and parents at individual schools have been involved in designing plans to relieve the overcrowding. Year-round school schedules have been one solution. Ninety-five schools have developed a year-round schedule. School planning teams have a high degree of self-determination. As a result, fifty-five schools are on a 45–15 schedule, nine schools are on a 90–30 schedule, fifteen schools are on a schedule called Concept-6, five schools are on a modified Concept-6 schedule, one school is on a 60–20 schedule, six schools are on a single-track 45–15 schedule, and three schools are on a continuous schedule.

Modified schedules must be prepared for year-round schools to meet four criteria: Answer documents must be scored with others of the same type and grade on the regular schedule. The year-round schedule may begin any time before the regular schedule if testing materials are available. The year-round schedule may end up to one week later than the regular schedule. Finally, year-round schools are to note the week of instruction when testing is scheduled in the regular schools and not depart more than a few weeks from that time in scheduling their own testing. Within these constraints, year-round schools are encouraged to develop testing schedules that fit the attendance patterns of the various attendance tracks at each school.

Problems of Interaction. Procedures developed over the years to ensure complete and reliable test results in a very large school district are the same procedures that make it difficult to afford flexibility to the year-round schools. If there were only a few schools, it would not be a problem to test each school during the same week of instruction, to scan the tests whenever they were ready, and to combine the resulting records later in the computer before the reports were produced. Unfortunately, the district does not have sufficient personnel to handle split jobs successfully at this time, either in scoring centers or at computer facilities.

The compromise — slight time adjustment to the testing schedule for year-round schools — causes many problems. Schools complain that they often must test students in the two weeks just before students leave for intersession or immediately after students return from a three- to eight-week vacation. A school with four different attendance tracks can face as many as four different testing schedules for each test administered. (Greater district flexibility would heighten this problem rather than relieve it.)

Another problem area is that year-round schools need test results sooner than regular schools do, since their school year begins on July 1. The system of test scoring suited to regular schools, which has the safety valve of summer processing and data return to schools in Spetember, does not fit year-round schools. Test data are needed much earlier if students and teachers at year-round schools are to benefit from them. Central office staff make sure that year-round schools receive test data as soon as they are processed, but this is not always as soon as they are needed.

A solution to some of these problems is now under study. Under this solution, the number of year-round school types would be limited to two. More individualization of schedules would then be possible as well as split processing and scoring.

Reporting of Results

Informal Reports. Pupil and school test results are available to individual schools as soon as they are produced. Results for the norm-referenced and competence tests scored by the district are available about six weeks after testing. State CAP test results, which only report school averages, do not become available to schools until six to eight months after testing.

Formal reports on district testing programs are presented first to the district board of education. The test information is not considered public information until after the board presentation. The board presentation occurs after schools have reviewed their own test data and any errors have been corrected. Usually, this occurs late in the fall semester. Concurrent with or shortly after presentation of test results to the board, formal reports are published and made available to the public. Until the board presentation, requests from the public for test data are filled with published reports from the preceding year.

Until formal, published reports are produced, test data are provided to district personnel for information and decision making in a variety of ways. The superintendent and the Office of Instruction receive a memo containing preliminary district test data as soon as they become available. The memo also describes trends and points out any unusual or unexpected aspects of the data. Wider distribution of preliminary test data occurs through the network of regional directors of instruction. Research and Evaluation Branch staff hold workshops for these regional leaders early in the fall semester. Each regional leader receives test data for region schools, and proper test interpretation is reviewed. Problem areas from the previous year are discussed at these meetings, and plans to reduce or avoid the problems in the coming year are made.

Formal Reports. For many years, the Research and Evaluation Branch published a single annual report that contained school-by-school norm-references test results — median and quartile national norm percentile scores — together with a discussion and interpretive aids. Since competence testing was added to the district's testing program, the annual publication also reports these data, together with district and school-by-school results for secondary schools and district averages only for elementary grades.

The California Assessment Program has been in existence for many years, but until very recently it seemed to receive little public notice or district use. The California State Department of Education held a press conference in November to release statewide average scores — often before individual districts received their school and district reports — and a board informative report was prepared by the district testing unit to alert the district superintendent and board members to the average district scores. No school-by-school public report was published, although school data were made available to newspapers or individuals who inquired. In recent years, the media and the public at large have taken an increasing interest in CAP school scores. Fortunately, the advance computer listings of school scores now available have made it possible for all scores to be presented to the district board in advance of the state's November press conference. Copies of the listings can now be made available to the media through the district's public information office at the same time that statewide results are made public.

Summary and Conclusion

A complex system of testing is operating successfully in a large urban school district. While the complexity of testing programs, schedules, and students still creates some problems, the professionalism and commitment of staff make all these testing programs work.

Floraline Stevens is director of the Research and Evaluation Branch, Los Angeles Unified School District.

Marilyn Burns is the assistant director; she is in charge of the district's testing unit.

*This large urban school district aims to provide a comprehensive
and accurate measurement system for teaching.*

A Case Study: Testing in the Dallas Independent School District

Cordelia R. Alexander

The systemwide testing program of the Dallas Independent School District is designed to support instruction with accurate test information. The characteristics and needs of the school district have determined the specific qualities of its testing program. Approximately 128,000 students are enrolled in district schools. Twenty-six percent of the students are white, 50 percent are black, and 22 percent are Hispanic. The district has thirty-four high schools, twenty-two middle schools, and one hundred twenty-seven elementary schools. More than 6,000 teachers serve in these schools, which extend across three subdistricts that are distinct in geographical location and administrative operations. The three subdistricts report directly to the general superintendent. This case study documents the major components of test implementation in the Dallas Independent School District.

Testing Program

The systemwide testing program administers a number of major tests: the Texas Assessment of Basic Skills (TABS), the Assessment of Baseline Curriculum (ABC) survey in English and Spanish versions, the ABC classroom tests, the Comprehensive Tests of Basic Skills–Español (CTBS-Español), the Language Assessment Scales (LAS) in English and Spanish versions, and

W. E. Hathaway (Ed.). *Testing in the Schools.* New Directions for Testing and Measurement, no. 19. San Francisco: Jossey-Bass, September 1983.

various district-adopted norm-referenced tests. These tests serve five educational functions: accountability, diagnosis and placement, parent conference information, interim and postinstruction assessment, and summative program evaluation.

The district is now in the middle of a five-year instructional improvement process. One aspect of this process involves the establishment of standards for student learning at each grade level. These standards will be a subset of the baseline curriculum. A student's performance in relation to these objectives will be used as a guideline in determining promotion or retention. A second aspect of the instructional improvement process involves the use of a district-developed testing system. The testing component is the Assessment of the Baseline Curriculum (ABC), which consists of two major products: the ABC classroom tests, which teachers use on an optional basis to gather information for making day-to-day instructional decisions, and the ABC survey tests, which have an attendant reporting system that can used to standardize measurement of students' performance in relation to promotion standards.

As established by the Texas Education Agency (TEA), TABS is a criterion-referenced measure administered to eligible students in grades 3, 5, and 9. Guidelines for the testing of special student populations and general administrative procedures are implemented according to TEA specifications. With the exception of certain special education students, all students at the targeted grade levels are expected to participate. Results of TABS are currently processed by Westinghouse Information Systems of Iowa City, Iowa, the agency contracted by TEA; all school and total district tests reports are returned to the district testing unit in May.

The LAS is an individually administered oral language measure used for instructional placement and evaluation. The CTBS–Español provides summative evaluation information for students who have been identified as limited-English-proficient (LEP) and who are enrolled in a Spanish language-based instructional program. The norm-referenced Iowa Tests of Basic Skills (ITBS) are used to assess students enrolled in kindergarten and grades 1 through 8. The Tests of Achievement and Proficiency (TAP) are administered to students enrolled in grades 9 through 11. The ITBS and TAP measure a full range of achievement and provide comparisons against which student progress can be judged.

Organizational Aspects

The systemwide testing group is part of the Department of Research, Evaluation, and Information Systems. Testing staff consist of nine personnel: one coordinator-manager, one principal analyst-programmer, three evaluators, and four clerical specialists. One evaluator and two clerical persons operate the test distribution center. It is the major responsibility of this group to cooperate with other departments in the school district and to establish effective communication and working relationships with the district's 183 schools.

Scheduling. At the beginning of each school year, a schedule of testing dates and general procedures for administering tests on a districtwide basis are approved and disseminated to all school personnel. The LAS is administered in the fall and the spring; the TABS occur in February; and the norm-referenced measures, the ABC survey, and the CTBS–Español are administered in the spring.

Test Coordinators and Training. The most important element in preparation for each year's program is the selection of a test coordinator by each school principal. At larger schools, more than one test coordinator is selected in order to expedite the testing program. Test coordinators in elementary schools are usually classroom teachers. In a few cases, this responsibility has been assigned to elementary counselors and other school administrators. In middle schools and high schools, a counselor normally serves as test coordinator. The test coordinator serves as an essential link between the systemwide testing group and the individual school by organizing, training, and implementing the testing program at the local school site. All school principals are routinely informed on testing matters through newsletters, memoranda, and meetings.

Five different groups of principals and test coordinators attend one or two training sessions during the school year. Participants are grouped by grade level and subdistrict assignment. The sessions relate to test administration procedures, district test policy, level assignments or restrictions for certain tests (ITBS, TAP, CTBS–Español), test security, and receipt and return of test materials. Special preparation is necessary for administration of the state-mandated TABS. The TABS district coordinator attends an annual workshop conducted by the Texas Education Agency and returns to the district to train the principals and test coordinators. Test coordinators and school principals receive a handbook before major testing activities begin. The handbook serves as a guide for implementing all tests administered through the systemwide testing group.

Students. Under district policy, all students take district-required tests with the exception of students exempted under guidelines related to special education and limited-English-proficient students. In aggregating test results for a school, test scores of some students enrolled in special education classes are included, while the scores of subtest areas in which a student receives special services are not aggregated. However, an individual report is produced for any special education or LEP student who is tested.

Special Services. The systemwide testing group provides various special services, which can be categorized into four broad areas: staff development sessions, individual conferences or contacts, a newsletter, and custom computer-generated reports. More than 100 staff development sessions are provided to school faculties annually. Test information is also provided to parents, school administrators, curriculum specialists, preservice teachers, and members of the community. On an annual basis, the Educational Administration and Supervision Area Test of the National Teacher Examinations is administered to approximately 200 candidates for the district's leadership training program. Throughout the school year, systemwide testing staff are available to respond to the questions and concerns of individual schools. Many hours are spent in individual conferences with test coordinators, principals, counselors, deans of instruction, and instructional specialists. Topics of discussion include test reports, parent topics, test score interpretation, and staff development planning. Fall and spring issues of a newsletter called *Checkpoint* are distributed to test coordinators, counselors, teachers, school principals, school administrators, P.T.A. members, and the school board. Approximately 700 copies are printed of each issue. Custom computer-generated services are provided to schools as resources permit.

Scoring and Reporting. All tests are scored or processed through the district's data-processing department. The systemwide testing analyst develops the computer software needed for scoring the tests, maintaining the data bases, and generating test reports. Test reports include class and grade-level listings of scores, student and parent reports, pressure-sensitive labels, and instructional skills analyses.

Distribution of Materials and Quality Control. The systemwide testing distribution center disseminates all the tests that are administered. Practice tests are also sent to district schools. The materials disseminated include test booklets and such materials as manuals, answer sheets, group testing headers, practice manuals, LAS cassette tapes, and practice answer sheets and the various test reports.

The emphasis of quality control is twofold: maintaining materials and ensuring the accuracy of data to be machine-scored, and monitoring the test procedures. All nonconsumable test booklets are assigned to schools according to the permanent numbers marked on each test booklet. On their return to the test distribution center, the booklets are verified, and those missing are noted. Answer sheets used in grades 3 through 11 are precoded with student identification information. This procedure has greatly improved the efficiency of test processing. As personnel become available, some test sessions are monitored by trained observers.

Out-of-Level Testing

Standardized tests have been criticized because grade-level tests have not seemed appropriate in content for students who score at the lower and upper extremes on such tests. Dallas students are no different from students in most large urban school districts in reflecting wide differences in achievement within grades. In order to meet the district's goals for instructional support, the systemwide testing group has implemented out-of-level testing since the

Iowa Tests of Basic Skills began to be used in 1974. The concept of out-of-level testing refers to the testing of students at functioning achievement levels regardless of grade placement.

Beginning in fall 1974 and continuing into the fall 1975 testing period, the ITBS was administered to entire grade-level classifications across grades 2 through 8 on an out-of-level basis. The test-level designations were based on the average achievement level of the grade-level group of students previously tested in the school. No school was directed to administer the ITBS more than two levels below actual grade level. High numbers of invalid and chance scores were reported from early use of the ITBS. Recognizing this problem, functional-level testing was implemented on an individual student basis across grade levels 4 through 8 in fall 1976. This procedure has continued in use to this day. Under this procedure, the content and difficulty level of the test assigned to an individual student are appropriate to the student's academic functional level. Test levels recommended for students currently enrolled in grades 4 through 8 are based on their ITBS achievement in reading and mathematics for the preceding year. Specifically, the average raw score percentage across both subtests is obtained, and the level is assigned according to the previous test level taken and scored within a defined reliable range. In general, reliable scores are defined as average raw score percentages of 30 to 80 percent of total test items.

Over the years, the number of students tested according to grade assignment has increased. Thus, the current test-level assignment procedures have provided generally accurate measurement, and they have permitted longitudinal tracking of higher achievement for students in grades 2 through 8. In spring 1982, more than 90 percent of the students in grades 2 and 3 were tested with the corresponding grade-level test. For that reason, both grades will be tested with the grade-level test in spring 1983. In spring 1982, more than 60 percent of the students in grades 4, 5, and 6 were tested with grade-level and above-grade-level tests. In grades 7 and 8, more than 50 percent of the students were tested according to grade-level classification.

In summary, the ITBS test-level assignments are restricted at each grade level in grades 4 through 8. Prior to test implementation, the recommendations of systemwide testing group staff reviewed and changed as needed by each school's teaching staff. Students who have no previous test results take the grade-level test. Students in kindergarten and grades 1, 2, 3, 9, 10, and 11 are tested according to grade-level assignment.

Summary and Conclusions

The required tests implemented through the Dallas systemwide testing program provide information that supports the instructional program by identifying student needs, effecting curricular changes, monitoring student learning, and communicating student needs and successes to the community. There will be changes in test implementation that indicate a continuing effort to ensure that data are valid and reliable. Accurate data will affect instruction positively both by determining what is known about a subject and by evaluating what has been learned.

The district's existing testing procedures indicate that four recommendations need to be considered and perhaps to be implemented. First, in order to further streamline the systemwide testing program, school personnel should participate in training that encourages proper use and interpretation of test results. The systemwide testing group staff can provide such training on request. Second, to ensure proper test implementation and effective use of test data, the link between the systemwide testing office and school test coordinators must be strengthened. Third, data for kindergarten and grades 1 and 2 will be more reliable if small test groupings (twelve to fifteen students) are introduced. Procedures that use the public address system to administer tests establish less than adequate rapport between the examiner and students. Some schools have already asked systemwide testing to monitor the extent to which proper testing procedures are being implemented. Finally, the practice tests and test-taking instructions that are now available must be fully used, especially in kindergarten and grades 1 through 3. Students in grade 3 must be provided with experience in the use of a separate answer sheet for a reasonable length of time prior to spring testing.

Cordelia R. Alexander has been coordinator of districtwide testing, Dallas (Texas) Independent School District, for the last six years. She has also served as evaluator of federal programs and as research scientist in institutional research projects for the district.

Can a useful program of achievement testing be conducted with a minimum of lost instructional time? Can the clerical burden on teachers also be minimized? These are goals of Austin's systemwide testing staff.

A Case Study: Testing in the Austin Independent School District

Glynn D. Ligon
M. Kevin Matter

A phenomenon that we have witnessed in our experiences at national conferences and with evaluation periodicals is that every system or program sounds better when it is described than it proves to be in practice. That is the disclaimer with which we preface this description of our testing program. Austin's systemwide testing program works well for us, but we are still striving to improve it. However, instead of describing our testing program and how it operates in detail, we will discuss some basic elements of the program adopted by the Austin Independent School District, which serves 55,000 students.

Procedures

What procedural elements make Austin's systemwide testing program an interesting case study? There are four key factors. First, the level of central orchestration and control is high. Surprisingly, the acceptance of central control has been very positive at the campus level. The trade-offs for principals and teachers have been tremendous savings in their time and the assurance that test scores from different schools are comparable.

Second, the Office of Research and Evaluation is committed to limiting the amount of instructional time devoted to standardized testing during the

W. E. Hathaway (Ed.). *Testing in the Schools.* New Directions for Testing and Measurement, no. 19. San Francisco: Jossey-Bass, September 1983.

school year. All evaluations and research studies are limited to using the systemwide testing data collected once a year in the spring. Only very limited achievement testing is done in addition to the annual systemwide effort, and most of this testing incorporates sampling, hired testers, or both in order to reduce the impact on schools.

Third, an in-house processing and reporting procedure has cut reporting time to a fraction of what it was four years ago. There are two keys to this reduction: dedicated computer time, during which we do not have to compete with payroll and other top-priority tasks, and a complete redesign of the computer programs to make scoring and reporting much more efficient.

Fourth, there is ample communication between school staff and testing staff. The telephone line to the testing office is always open, the schools know it, and they use it. Testing staff accept all invitations to speak to faculties and plan needed training for all teachers, principals, and building test coordinators.

Philosophy

The operating philosophy that guides our testing program has five basic parts. First, standardized tests provide important information for decision making at all levels. Second, timely and accurate reporting is necessary to allow optimum use of results from standardized tests. Third, for standardized testing to fulfill its role in the school system, every aspect of testing, from selection of tests to use of results, must be of concern to testing staff. Fourth, saving instructional time and teacher's planning time necessitates limiting the clerical tasks that teachers must perform. Fifth, accountability is the major function of the testing program; however, providing related services to school staff in the interpretation and use of results must also be emphasized.

Staffing

The testing staff needed to implement this operating philosophy successfully consists of a senior evaluator, an evaluator, three evaluation assistants, one full-time and a half-time programmer, and a secretary. The fact that the Director of the Office of Research and Evaluation reports directly to the Superintendent serves to maintain the independence and objectivity of testing staff. Reports are issued through the Superintendent without any editing by school system staff.

The primary justification for testing staff is the time savings for school personnel that result from the efficient, centralized testing operation. In the final analysis, the resources invested in testing staff pay dividends in the reduced load on teachers. How testing is organized to relieve teachers from some test-related duties will be discussed later. At this point, it is appropriate to detail some of the characteristics of an effective systemwide testing staff. We select or train staff to exhibit these critical characteristics: They anticipate issues, requests, and material needs so that crises can be avoided. Issues are resolved through proper channels of authority, and the resolutions are documented in writing. Teachers' and principals' comments and concerns are sought, and each concern is answered. Roles are clearly specified in writing for parents, students, teachers, counselors, principals, testing staff, and administrators. Staff never assume that a role is clear, that a report is self-explanatory, or that reminders are unnecessary. Drafts of forms, procedures, and reports are reviewed by all groups affected. Suggestions are considered, but the final decisions are based on maximizing validity while maintaining the usefulness of results. Finally, accuracy receives the highest priority.

Activities of Systemwide Testing Staff

An extensive list of responsibilities naturally goes along with such an all-inclusive testing plan. We sort out the various elements of this plan by their timing: before testing, during testing, and after testing. Before testing, staff select tests, levels, and forms; determine exemptions and special testing procedures; specify test preparation activities for students; train staff to administer tests and handle testing materials; select testing dates and times; and deliver testing materials to schools. During testing, staff monitor classrooms, selected at random, and troubleshoot to remedy problem situations. After testing, systemwide testing staff inventory materials, processing booklets and answer sheets, update missing and incorrect information, report results, and train school and district staff to interpret results.

Materials and Testing

Three main categories of materials facilitate testing on campuses. To keep everyone up-to-date on testing schedules and pending events and to provide answers to current questions, a newsletter called *Nuts and Bolts of Testing* is published as needed. One of the first conclusions that we reached in our efforts to coordinate testing across a large number of campuses is that if one person asks a question, then many others have asked, will ask, or should ask the same question. The newsletter has been used both as a quick response medium when an issue is urgent and as a timely reminder just before critical events are due to occur.

Teachers administer standardized tests to the students in their classrooms. To prepare teachers for administering these tests, they receive packets that contain scripts for talks with students and checklists that detail what the teacher must do for the testing step by step. Finally, each campus has a designated building test coordinator. These building test coordinators, who usually are counselors or principals, are the contact persons for all test-related matters. Training is provided to test coordinators directly and to teachers through them. Test coordinators receive material inventories, checklists, and all testing materials for their school from systemwide testing staff.

Processing Test Booklets and Answer Sheets

Seven years ago, when the Office of Research and Evaluation first took over the systemwide testing program, processing and reporting were accomplished by a combination of hand scoring by teachers and the publisher's scoring service. After four years of local processing using school system hardware and software, turnaround time had been reduced to four weeks. Three years ago, in an attempt to reduce both turnaround time and reporting errors to a minimum, extensive changes were made. The outcome has been Friday-to-Monday turnaround for any test taken with separate machine-scannable answer sheets and two-week turnaround for tests that require students to mark answers in the test booklet. The two-week turnaround includes the time that it takes to transport test booklets to a school district that has an optical scanner that can handle booklets.

This dramatic improvement coincided with a major change in the tests and with the introduction of out-of-level testing. Ironically, both factors actually contributed to the improvement by providing an opportunity to throw out the old processing programs and to design a new, more efficient system. What are the characteristics of this new processing system and the other changes that were made three years ago? First, the computer program written to score the tests was designed to accomplish in one process what had taken several steps in the past. The tests are scored and normed, skill area scores are calculated, and critical errors, such as students' taking invalid test levels, are identified in a single sequence. The real beauty of the new program, however, is that most of the hand sorting that used to be required before answer sheets could be scanned has been eliminated. The computer program does not require answer sheets to be in any particular order, and both test levels and grade levels can be mixed in the same batch. The savings in school staff and testing staff time have been remarkable.

Second, the key to not having to sort answer sheets is the locally designed answer sheet formats, which appear to the optical scanner to have a single format, although the answer sheet for each tests level appears to be different. Test level is coded onto each sheet, and this triggers scoring from the appropriate tables.

Third, information that is not essential is not coded on students' answer sheets or booklets. In many other school districts, teachers must code each student's birthdate, sex, and ethnicity on students' answer sheets before a test can be processed. All this information has been eliminated from the test processing. It is picked up from other files in the computer at a later time.

Fourth, the information that is required is precoded on each student's answer sheet by the computer, or it is bubbled in by hand onto test booklets by hourly workers hired for the task. The primary benefit of this procedure is time saved for teachers. A secondary benefit is the greatly increased accuracy of the resulting information.

Fifth, anything that can be done in advance in done in advance, and anything that can be done afterwards is done afterwards. This leaves the critical time when the tests are being processed as free as possible.

Finally, one of the most critical factors is the scheduling of test processing to assure dedicated computer time. This means that testing staff must work until 3:00 A.M. to finish scanning answer sheets so that the programmer can begin at 8:00 A.M. on Saturday morning to process the data. Uncontested computer time is tremendously productive for producing reports. The bottom line is that answer sheets for grades 3 through 12 are delivered to the testing office on the Friday after testing, and the reports are hand-delivered to schools on the following Monday morning. For testing staff, a tough weekend of work accomplishes the equivalent of four weeks of work during regular working hours.

Security

The security of test booklets has become a major issue in Austin. One of the factors that influenced the changes in testing procedures introduced three years ago was the widespread access that teachers and students had to the tests. To protect our substantial investment in the new test, the inventory system has been substantially tightened. But, controlling our own booklets was only part of the problem. So many teachers, parents, and students have access to test booklets through libraries and test publishers that some special steps had to be taken. University libraries in the area agreed to restrict their test copies to reference areas from which tests could not be checked out and where they could not easily be duplicated. The test publisher agreed not to honor any orders from Austin school district personnel without the approval of district testing staff. Today, security is better, but we are constnatly finding other sources of tests, such as the free copies given out at displays at conferences.

Evaluation of Testing

We have just begun to give schools report cards on their efficiency in testing and in the handling of test materials. Our first attempt was to list schools that were "perfect" in their handling of test materials in a newsletter. To our surprise, the schools took this so seriously that the schools that had not been listed wanted to know in what respect they were inadequate. Now, after each testing effort, schools receive a report card — actually a checklist that gives them specifics about the neatness, completeness, and timeliness of their efforts. The reaction from principals and building test coordinators has been neutral to positive. Testing staff appreciate the chance to document problems passed on to them by schools. Overall, most schools receive a pat on the back for a job well done that previously went unrecognized.

Test Results and Their Use

Test results need to be timely, but they must be presented clearly and concisely in order to be useful. In Austin, test scores are used as criteria for placement in several junior and senior high school courses and for meeting the district's minimum competence requirement for high school graduation. Students and parents receive test scores on a label affixed to a brochure that briefly describes the test and how the scores are used. School personnel receive several listings (student alphabetical, rank order, and so forth) to aid in course placement. Junior and senior high school teachers are provided with classroom achievement summaries of their students for each period of the day. Principals receive school summary scores for skill areas and for subtest areas in relation to national norms. School, district, and national averages are included in the reports for principals, which can be used to develop and assess school goals. These test reports are reviewed annually by testing staff, and input is solicited from school personnel on improvements that can be made in the test reporting system.

Summary and Conclusions

Despite the wishes of some, there appears never to be a conclusion to a systemwide testing effort. The broad scope of the responsibilities handled by Austin's testing staff makes systemwide testing a year-long cycle, which starts all over again just as soon as one year's tasks are completed.

The best summary of Austin's systemwide achievement testing effort is that every aspect of testing, from the selection of tests to the use of results, has been carefully planned to maximize the validity and reliability of results. A high level of centralized orchestration of testing has resulted in savings of instructional time and improved the comparability of results across classrooms, schools, and programs. Although achievement testing is still far from being a popular activity with teachers and principals, it is now much less of a burden, and we hope, much more of a reliable information source for decision making in Austin.

Glynn D. Ligon is senior evaluator for the Austin (Texas)
Independent School District, where he supervises the systemwide
achievement and minimum competency testing program.

M. Kevin Matter is the evaluator for Austin's systemwide
achievement and minimum competency testing programs.

By using criterion-referenced testing as one aspect of a program evaluation requirement, Mississippi is basing instructional improvement on student performance.

A Case Study: Testing in the State of Mississippi

Thomas H. Saterfiel

Mississippi has suffered with the rest of the nation from the public's general loss of faith in the public school systems. The public demands stringent accountability. One of the problems with accountability is that every state uses the same term with a different definition. Some states have enacted minimum competence laws and some have established graduation requirements, while others have instituted massive testing programs. In building the plans for the state of Mississippi, two distinct decisions were made.

The first decision was that accountability in the state of Mississippi should be a process that addresses improved student achievement. The second decision was that the plan needed to be one that changed people. It would be very easy for the state of Mississippi to write the perfect curriculum or perfect test or to pass a state law which said that ignorance was no longer allowed. It is much more difficult to change teachers, principals, school boards, and communities so that improved student achievement is really valued. In order to change people, a system had to be designed to involve people — to allow them to play a major role in designing and implementing any plan of accountability. Therefore, while the structure and the policies were established at the state level, the main impetus for carrying out, approving, and implementing the accountability plan in the state of Mississippi was located at the local school district level.

W. E. Hathaway (Ed.). *Testing in the Schools.* New Directions for Testing and Measurement, no. 19. San Francisco: Jossey-Bass, September 1983.

Given these two decisions, there was no doubt that it would take longer to develop good plans than it had in other states. In addition, at least initially, individual schools might develop systems that were less than perfect. Mississippi gambled that a slow, orderly change that involved people might also bring about relatively permanent and lasting change.

Basic Orientation

Like many other parts of the country, Mississippi has attempted to discover the perfect textbook and the perfect curriculum many times over, only to find that, after the package has been bought, the student still fails to learn. So, while the state of Mississippi seeks to provide a sufficient foundation for developing individual school curricula, it will not try to delineate specific behavioral objectives on a day-by-day or a week-by-week basis for each school teacher. Local school districts will be expected to take the leadership role on curriculum.

There will be a need for some systematic data on students to help districts to make those decisions. The Mississippi Education Reform Act of 1982 ordered the State Department of Education to test every child in grades, 3, 5, 8, and 11 in the basic skills areas. It further required the State Department of Education to establish minimum standards for schools and school districts for their students' performance, including criteria for assigning grades, determining promotion, and graduating from high school. However, the state does not make individual decisions about student grades, promotion, or graduation requirements. Schools or school districts that are found to be lacking in terms of the minimum standards will be cited publicly, and they will receive assistance from the state of Mississippi to help them to improve their instructional program.

The final and most important part of Mississippi's accountability law began in 1979, when the Mississippi Accreditation Commission established two new standards to implement a program that has come to be known as the Accountability and Instructional Management (AIM) plan. Mississippi educators believed that an accountability program should emphasize more than minimum competence in basic skills. In addition, too many states have found that an emphasis on minimum competencies got them the minimums but no more.

The state of Mississippi therefore decided to include the entire instructional program. In addition, it realized that there must be a system to monitor the program. Instead of creating a new system or relying on one statewide test to make the necessary decisions, Mississippi chose to use the state accreditation commission, which already had a well-developed procedure and a solid structure for functioning within the state of Mississippi. The standards that were implemented under the AIM plan led accreditation to mandate that a school in the state of Mississippi had to have an active instructional management program in order to meet minimum accrediting standards. In essence, the standards ordered a program evaluation review to be conducted on an annual basis on each curriculum area. The plan is scheduled to be implemented on November 1, 1984.

Many of the ideas associated with the AIM plan that will be presented here are very straightforward and familiar to educators. The unique piece that was placed into the accrediting standards dealt with the role of testing. There is no way in which decisions about instructional programs can be based on student achievement unless a school district has some sort of systematic testing for students concerning the goals and objectives that have been developed for the curriculum.

Some argue that the AIM plan is too expensive, that it takes too much time, and that it requires too much testing. However, every school district in the state of Mississippi had already told the people that it had an instructional management plan called a course of study. The problem was, no one had ever defined what a course of study should do, and few had suggested that it should be used in the classroom once it was written. There was also a standard for accreditation which said that every student should be tested regularly in terms of the goals and objectives of the instructional program. However, that standard was rarely considered by a school during self-study.

The testing standard was rather simple. The accreditation commission simply said that students would be expected to be measured at least once a year in terms of the objectives stated in the course of study. That evaluation might take the form of teacher-made tests, performance situations, checklists, or any other evaluation instrument that collected data concerning student performance on the stated objectives. The key was that the faculty, administration, and school board would take a look at least once a year at students' performance in terms of the objectives that they had established as important for the courses and grade levels that the district offered to students.

The state of Mississippi will not be involved in passing, failing, or handing out diplomas to individuals except as these issues relate to general policy. The local school districts are going to have to decide what they can accept and live with. Given the limited funds available to accomplish this task statewide, it was quite obvious that the plans developed in Mississippi must develop slowly over time, that they must become an integral part of daily classroom activity, and that they must have the total support of teachers, administrators, and the local community in the school district.

Major Components

The course of study, which had always been a requirement under accreditation, was defined by the AIM plan to have at least two parts. The first part was an outline called the program design. The program design was a simple working document that the district could use to better describe the program and to better communicate with parents who did not have the time or the inclination to deal with the jargon that educators used.

The second part of the plan was called the program description. The program description addressed only three audiences, using a simple input-process-output system. The outputs were the student objectives — the student behaviors that teachers felt they needed to see to be certain that a student had mastered a particular subject matter area. The process was directed at methodology. It described the kind of classroom activities, homework, presentation patterns, and detailed information that had proved to be useful to successful teachers in accomplishing the objectives. Many times, the process statements were actually simple behavioral objectives (enabling objectives): the kind of classroom preparatory activities that allowed students to deal with the larger, more complicated concepts (terminal objectives).

The third part of the plan, inputs, dealt mainly with preconditions and resources. It is unreasonable to expect a teacher to teach a course that requires resources for laboratory work if none are available. In addition, it is impossible to expect a teacher to prepare a student to work in an advanced course when there are no requirements for the student to learn minimum competencies in previous courses. Description of the course of study was not new to many school districts, but many school districts found nonetheless that they had to go back and rethink their entire instructional program.

Again, systematic testing was the key to making the system work. Educators never had much problem in writing down interesting things for children to do, but when they went to the classroom, they often reinterpreted those objectives to mean whatever they wanted them to mean, even if they thought the objectives had been written in so specific a form that no one could misunderstand them. By ordering systematic testing for each objective, the AIM plan required data to be collected at the local level to demonstrate the achievement of students in terms of the instructional program.

The next requirement of the system is for the district to establish standards for student performance based on the evaluation system that it has selected. These standards were designed to identify when a program was failing to deliver the kind of achievement by students that the teaching faculty expected. The next step in the program was to collect student achievement data. As already noted, student achievement data came not only from paper-and-pencil tests but from a wide range of evaluation information, which could be placed in a systematic reporting system to identify strengths and weaknesses in the program. Once the data had been placed against the standards that had been established, discrepancies between the standards and the performance could be identified. Areas where weaknesses existed would be the areas that received major emphasis during the following year.

Each district would have to establish an improvement plan for eliminating the discrepancies that emerged in this process. This plan may deal with changing the structure of the curriculum, changing the expectations, improving the teachers' in-service training, or any other activity that faculty believe can lead to improved student achievement. The school district was required by law to report annually to the public concerning the students' achievement. Obviously, any changes made in the program as the result of identification of discrepancies would then become part of the new AIM plan, which would be reviewed again in the following year, thereby creating an ongoing program evaluation system.

Accreditation said, "If these are the objectives that you have said you want students to do, then test them. If you do not want to test those objectives, then do not put them down." The accrediting commission believed that those standards, while simple, were reasonable and that they could provide a foundation for efforts by individuals in the school district to make the instructional program the most important part of judging and evaluating the school system.

Requirements for Success

Two of the major requirements for success in implementing the kind of instructional program outlined in Mississippi are money and time. There is only a limited amount of time available in the school day. School boards have to make some major decisions to allow teachers time to discuss the content of courses and the standards that need to be established. It often takes money to provide that kind of time — money for substitute teachers, money for teachers to be able to work when students are not present.

A third requirement is training for principals and coordinators in curriculum planning and instructional management. We have trained an entire generation of principals to believe that they are the instructional leaders of their school, but they have had few demonstrations of what an instructional leader actually does.

Another major criticism of the AIM plan in Mississippi has been that teachers cannot develop the kind of quality tests that are necessary to make these decisions. That sounds like a good criticism until somebody realized that teachers have been using their own tests with no supervision to make exactly those kinds of decisions as long as public schools have existed. No doubt there needs to be improvement; no doubt surveys of teacher-made tests in the state of Mississippi have identified tremendous deficiencies. But, we simply do not say that we have stopped testing students because we have found that teachers do not do a good job.

Technological support does not suggest that each individual teacher will be expected to become a proficient professional test writer. However, it does suggest that, when we find individuals who have a talent for developing good tests, we will train them and give them the support that it takes to make them able to help the rest of the faculty design the kinds of tests that will help them to make decisions.

Finally, success will require that there be sharing among practitioners.

The people who know how best to implement an instructional management program are the people who have implemented an instructional management program in their school. Individual districts will have to be willing to share their ideas, their failures, and their successes and maybe even their test items if they plan to succeed. A consortium of thirty school districts in Mississippi called the Program of Research and Evaluation for Public Schools is now in the process of developing a statewide test item banking system that will allow member school districts to share test items developed by local schools to measure the objectives that they have established for students. No doubt everything that is developed in one school will not be totally applicable in another, but what one district develops may provide ideas and assistance to another school district that is developing its own unique system.

Testing Is the Key

The one unique change that has been made in accrediting standards for the state of Mississippi lies in saying, "We must see some data that indicate that student achievement results from that course of study." The only way in which those kinds of data can be derived is by testing. Teachers and principals will have to be trained to use test data for making decisions. We tend to use many other factors to make decisions.

A second change that use of tests will produce is that student performance rather than time will have to be the criterion for moving a student through the curriculum. If a teacher decides that he or she is going to use achievements to move students, then the key decision-making element will be good tests. The tests will have to improve, and the teachers will have to place more confidence in the tests if we have such a system.

Tests will also be reviewed in addressing both student and program decisions. We are aware that tests can assist us in making decisions about the grade that a student will receive or about whether the student will pass the course. However, if a school expects to have an instructional management system, it must be able to make decisions about individual program components. The district must be able to know whether various general goals are being met by the program. Simply making a decision about one individual child does not address those kinds of decisions. Principals and teachers will have to be trained to realize that tests will play the major role in making the kinds of decisions that can lead to improvements in the instructional program.

Conclusion

The AIM plan does not promise to cure all the problems of education. It also does not promise to produce the best possible student achievement test or the best program for reading. The purpose of Mississippi's AIM plan is to involve faculty, principals, and school board members in a positive program for improvement. The purpose of the program is to make school boards and all the people who work for the school boards realize that the most important decision that a school district makes is the one that deals with student achievement. The most important piece of information that a school district decision maker can have concerns student achievement.

The AIM plan will take a long time to accomplish. It establishes the tools to manage for improvement. When you are trying to change a system, you do not ask experts to tell people why they need to change. The first step is for the people to realize that they need to change and to ask for assistance. Once the tools have been created and school districts have begun to make decisions concerning the instructional program, the positive moves necessary to improve instruction will occur.

The goals established for improvement in Mississippi are long-term goals. Mississippi is trying to move off the bottom of the pile. We have always had the dedicated teachers who are necessary to accomplish those tasks. All the literature on the effective teacher has also been reviewed. But, in the long run, if we are going to change, it will require more than just knowing what needs to be done and more than simply writing laws that say it must be done. Individual teachers in classrooms will have to do these things.

The key driving element in the AIM plan is the improvement of classroom tests. Unless we can relate testing directly to the primary emphasis of the instructional program in the classroom, testing is simply a tangent. The AIM plan in the state of Mississippi lays the kind of foundation that will make testing even more important, even more critical, and even more valuable in making educational improvement a reality in Mississippi.

Thomas H. Saterfiel is associate professor of educational psychology at Mississippi State University and director of the Program of Research and Evaluation for Public Schools (PREPS), a research and evaluation consortium of thirty public school districts in Mississippi.

Index

A

Ability, and testing, 43–44
Airasian, P. W., 8, 16
Albuquerque public schools: analysis of testing in, 79–84; department procedures in, 80–81; dissemination of results in, 81–84; evaluation services in, 81; and media coverage, 82–84; reorganization in, 79–80
Alexander, C. R., 91–96
Anderson, D. E., 23, 27
Anderson, G. E., 65–77
Anderson, J., 77
Apple II, 66
ASC, 86
Assembly Bill 65 (California), 86
Assessment of Baseline Curriculum (ABC), 91, 92, 93
Atari, 66
Austin Independent School District: analysis of testing in, 97–102; evaluation in, 101; materials in, 99; philosophy in, 98; procedures in, 97–98; processing in, 100–101; security in, 101; staffing in, 98–99; student preparation in, 19, 21, 22, 24, 26; test results in, 102

B

Baker, E. L., 7, 17
Basic Inventory of Natural Language (INL), 86
Beck, M., 8, 17
Beckum, L. C., 39–47
Bishop, C. H., 27
Black, H., 41, 47
Bloom, B. S., 31, 35, 37, 38
Boston, minority students in, 41
Boyd, J., 8, 17
Brown v. *Board of Education of Topeka*, 40
Burns, M., 85–89
Burry, L., 38
Busby, J., 72

C

California: intelligence testing in, 41–42; teacher certification testing in, 42–43
California Assessment Program (CAP), 85–86, 87, 88, 89
California State Department of Education, 89
Carelessness, and student preparation, 19, 20
Center for the Study of Evaluation, 7, 17; study by, 8–16
Chambers, B. A., 29–38
Clark, C. M., 17, 38
Classroom testing: adaptive, 69, 70, 76; and administration, 70; applications of microcomputers to, 65–77; assembly for, 68–69; future of, 76; item storage for, 67–68; and microcomputer technology, 66–67; score reporting and analysis for, 72–75; scoring for, 70–72
Cleveland, Ohio, teacher-made tests in, 30–37
Cline, A., 43, 47
Commodore PET, 66
Competence testing, and minority students, 42–43
Comprehensive Tests of Basic Skills (CTBS): compensatory and bilingual programs and, 86; district scoring of, 80
Comprehensive Tests of Basic Skills-Español, 86, 91, 92, 93
Confusion, and student preparation, 19–20, 21–22
Counseling, test data in, 44–45
Crouse, D. B., 72, 76

D

Dallas Independent School District: analysis of testing in, 91–96; organization of program in, 92–94; out-of-level testing in, 94–95; program in,

111

Dallas Independent School District: *(continued)* 91-92; recommendations in, 96; special services in, 93-94; test coordinators in, 93
Datta, L., 37, 38
Debra P. v. Turlington, 42
Dewitt, L. J., 69, 76
Diamond, J., 23, 26
Diana et al. v. California State Board of Education, 41
DIGITEK machine, 72
Dorr-Bremme, D. W., 7-17

E

Ebel, R. L., 15, 17, 27, 31, 37, 38
Educational Development Corporation, 72-75
Educational Testing Service, 71
Eichelberger, R. T., 24, 26
Epstein, R., 17
Essay questions, lack of, in teacher-made tests, 37
Evans, W., 23, 26

F

FAST system, 71
Flaugher, R. L., 44, 47
Fleming, M., 29-38
Florida, competence testing in, 42, 43
Flynn, J. T., 23, 27

G

Garcia-Quintana, R., 59, 64
Gleason, G. T., 66, 77
Goslin, D. A., 8, 17
Gould, S. J., 40, 47
Gronlund, N. E., 31, 38
Guessing: and latent trait analysis, 62; and student preparation, 20, 23

H

Hambleton, R. K., 65-77
Hamm, D. W., 59, 64
Hampton, S_H., 27
Hastings, J. T., 38
Hathaway, W. E., 1-3
Herman, J. L., 7-17
Hilloch, B. A., 17

Hills, J. R., 31, 35, 38
Hobsen v. Hansen, 41
Hoffman, B., 41, 47
Howse, G., 65, 77
Huron Institute, 7, 17

I

I.B.M., test scoring by, 70-71
Intelligence testing: background of, 40; misuse of, 41-42
Iowa Tests of Basic Skills (ITBS): and average scores, 24; in Dallas, 92, 93; and testwiseness, 23
Item bank, for classroom testing, 65, 67-68, 76
Item characteristic curves (ICCs), and item response theory, 60-63
Item forms, for classroom tests, 68-69
Item response theory: analysis of, 49-64; concept of, 49-50, 63; conclusion on, 63-64; estimating values for, 59-60; example of, 51-54; and item characteristic curves, 60-63; latent traits related to, 51-55; and microcomputers, 70

J

Jacobsen, K., 17
Jelden, D. L., 65, 77
Jencks, C., 45, 47
Jensen, A., 40
Jones, P., 21, 22, 23, 24, 27
Jongsma, E. A., 23, 27

K

Kelly, J. L., 17, 38
Koehler, R. A., 27
Kreit, L. H., 24, 27

L

Language Assessment Scales (LAS), 91, 92, 93, 94
Larry P. v. Riles, 41-42, 44
Latent trait analysis: analysis of theory of, 49-64; concept of, 49, 63; conclusion on, 63-64; discrimination parameter for, 61; estimating values for, 59-60; example of, 51-54; geometric representation for, 55-56; and guess-

ability, 62; item responses related to, 51–55; mathematical representation for, 56–58; measurement in, 55–59; one-parameter model for, 57–59; three-parameter model for, 62–63; two-parameter model for, 60–62
Lazar-Morrison, C., 29, 36, 38
Leary, M. E., 41, 47
Ligon, G. D., 19–27, 97–102
Lindquist/Rulon test scoring machine, 71
Lippey, G., 65, 77
Lord, F. M., 50, 64, 69, 70, 77
Los Angeles Unified School District: analysis of testing in, 85–89; multiple programs in, 85–86; multiple schedules in, 86–88; result reporting by, 88–89

M

McKenna, B. H., 17, 29, 38
McKinley, R. L., 69, 77
Madaus, G. F., 38
Marschall, L. A., 77
Matter, M. K., 3, 97–102
Measurement theories: on latent traits and item responses, 49–64; and unidimensionality, 50
Mehrens, W. A., 17, 37–38
Microcomputers: applications of, 65–77; concept of, 65, 77; deciding on, 66–67; future of, 76; item storage by, 67–68; technology of, 66–67; test administration by, 70; test assembly by, 68–69; test score reporting and analysis by, 72–75; test scoring by, 70–72
Millman, J., 22, 27, 68, 77
Minority students: analysis of testing and, 39–47; and competency testing, 42–43; concerns about, 41; conclusion on, 46; and expectations for testing, 45–46; and intelligence test misuse, 41–42; issues related to, 40–43; researchers' concerns about, 41; and test data use, 43–45
Mississippi: Accountability and Instructional Management (AIM) plan in, 104–109; accountability in, 103–105; analysis of testing in, 103–109; components of plan in, 105–107; conclusions on, 108–109; orientation of,

104–105; requirements for success in, 107–108; testing as key in, 108
Mississippi Accreditation Commission, 104
Mississippi Education Reform Act of 1982, 104
Morton, S. G., 39–40
Moy, R., 38
Murray, L. N., 65–77

N

National Assessment of Educational Progress, 37
National Defense Education Act, 40
National Institute of Education, 7n
National Merit Scholarship, 81
National Teacher Examination, Educational Administration and Supervision Area Test of, 94
N.C.S., and optical scanners, 72
Nero, B., 24, 27
New Mexico High School Proficiency Examination, scoring tapes for, 80
Novick, M. R., 64

O

OPSCAN Corporation, 72
Osborne, 66
Outlaw, W. S., 68, 77

P

PAIR, 86
Parents, preparation of, for standardized tests, 25–26
Peckham, R. F., 41–42
Peel, E. A., 24, 27
Perrone, V., 7, 17
Physical Performance Test (PPT), 86
Polin, L., 38
Popham, W. J., 67, 77
Porter, A. C., 17, 38
Practice tests, and student preparation, 23–24
Preliminary Scholastic Aptitude Test, scoring tapes for, 81
Principals: attitudes of, toward testing, 12–14; test results used by, 9–10, 12
Program of Research and Evaluation for Public Schools (PREPS), 108
Prophet, M., 5

Q

Quinto, F., 29, 38

R

Rasch, G., 58, 64
Reckase, M. D., 69, 77
Resnick, L. B., 8, 17
Robinson, C., 79-84
Rudman, H. C., 15, 17, 36, 38
Rudner, L. M., 17
Ryan, J. P., 49-64

S

Salmon-Cox, L., 8, 17
Salter, S., 43, 47
San Francisco, minority students in, 41
Saterfiel, T. H., 3, 103-109
SCANTRONICS, 72
Schaefer, E., 77
SCRIBE, 71
SHARP, 86
Skelly v. Wright, 41
Slakter, M. J., 23, 27
Southwest Regional Laboratory, 86
Spearman, C. E., 40
Stake, R. E., 17
Stanford Binet test, misuse of, 41
State Department of Education (Mississippi), 104
Stein, G., 43, 47
Stetz, F., 8, 17
Stevens, F., 85-89
Student preparation: analysis of, 19-27; and carelessness, 19, 20; and confusion, 19-20, 21-22; and guessing, 20, 23; literature review on, 22-24; philosophy for, 21; plan for, 21-22; and practice tests, 23-24; standardization of, 26; and test anxiety, 19, 20, 21; and test practice, 24; and testwiseness, 22-23; and time use, 20, 22
Students: causes of poor performance by, 19-20; minority, 39-47
Survey of Essential Skills (SES), 86

T

Teacher-made tests: analysis of, 29-38; background on, 29-30; behavioral categories in, 31-36; content review of, 31-32, 33-36; conclusions on, 36-38; essay questions lacking in, 37;

quality of, 15-16; technical review of, 30-31, 32-34
Teachers: assessment skills of, 15-16; attitudes of, toward testing, 12-14; certification tests for, 42-43; preparation of, for standardized tests, 24-25; test results used by, 11-12
Test anxiety, and student preparation, 19, 20, 21
Test practice, and student preparation, 24
Test results: constructive uses for, 43-45; decision making uses of, 9-12; dissemination of, 81-84
Testing: and ability, 43-44; advocates of, 7; in Albuquerque, 79-84; analysis of use of, 7-17; attitudes toward, 12-14; in Austin, 97-102; background on, 7-9; classroom, 65-77; conclusions on, 14-16; criticisms of, 7, 14; in Dallas, 91-96; expectations for, 45-46; intelligence, 40, 41-42; in Los Angeles, 85-89; and measurement theories, 49-64; and microcomputers, 65-77; and minority students, 39-47; in Mississippi, 103-109; needs met by, 39-40; qualities important in, 16; renewed interest in, 1; required, impact of, 15; standardized, preparation for, 19-27; teacher-made, 29-38
Tests of Achievement and Proficiency (TAP), 92, 93
Testwiseness, and student preparation, 22-23
Texas Assessment of Basic Skills (TABS), 91, 92, 93
Texas Education Agency (TEA), 92, 93
Time use, and student preparation, 20, 22
TOPICS, 86
TRS-80, 66
Tyler, R., 7, 17

U

Unidimensionality: concept of, 50; conclusions about, 54-55; testable hypotheses of, 56

W

Wanous, D. S., 17, 37-38
Warshauer, E., 23, 27
Wechsler test, misuse of, 41

Weiss, D. J., 69, 76, 77
Westinghouse Information Systems, 92
Wilkes, C., 71
Williams, R. L., 41, 47
Woellner, R. S., 15, 17
WRITE: Jr and Sr, 86

Y

Yashinsky, J., 17
Yeh, J. P., 15, 17, 29, 36, 38
Yerkes, R., 40